Briefly Considered
From the Mainstream

Notes and Observations on the Sources of Western Culture

JUDE P. DOUGHERTY

ST. AUGUSTINE'S PRESS
South Bend, Indiana

Manufactured in the United States of America

1 2 3 4 5 6   21 20 19 18 17 16 15

Library of Congress Cataloging in Publication Data
Dougherty, Jude P., 1930–n
Briefly considered : from the mainstream:
notes and observations on the sources of western culture /
Jude P. Dougherty. – 1st [edition].
pages cm
Includes bibliographical references and index.
ISBN 978-1-58731-081-2 (paperbound : alk. paper)
1. Philosophy, Ancient. 2. Philosophy, Medieval.
3. Science – Philosophy. 4. Islam. 5. Social problems. I. Title.
B181.D68 2013
190 – dc23   2013027535

∞ The paper used in this publication meets the minimum requirements of the American National Standard for Information Sciences Permanence of Paper for Printed Materials, ANSI Z39.481984.

ST. AUGUSTINE'S PRESS
www.staugustine.net

Acknowledgments

The author is grateful to the following for permission to reproduce previously published articles:

Modern Age for "Moderate Islam," "Two Treatises on the Acquisition and Use of Power," and "Property as a Condition of Liberty."

Toleranz und Mensohen Wuerde, published by Duncker und Humblot GmbH, Berlin, for "Tolerance: Virtue or Vice."

Briefly Considered

Other Books of Interest from St. Augustine's Press

Contents

Part III - Aids to the Understanding of Islam

Introduction

The mainstream finds its headwaters in antiquity if not in the pre-Socratics, certainly in Plato and Aristotle. Through the centuries that stream has been nourished by the Stoics, the Neoplatonists, the Scholastics, the Arab commentators, and the early moderns. Compatible with common sense, the philosophy of Aristotle was mastered and commented upon throughout the Middle Ages, informing in one way or another nearly every major treatise on nature, human nature, and things divine. Augustine, Anselm, Thomas, Scotus, and Bonaventure all drew upon antiquity. Though primarily theologians, in their appropriation of the Greek and Roman classics, they developed philosophies of their own, adding to the scholastic corpus. Platonic and Aristotelian themes merged in Aquinas to give us the notion of participation and a sense of the hierarchy of being. Boethius in his treatment of the Trinity is clearly an Aristotelian and Thomas's *Commentary on the De Trinitate of Boethius* is a classic itself, and in its analysis of human knowing provides the outline of a philosophy of science. The Aristotelian corpus prevailed through most of the Reformation and only began to be challenged in the late sixteenth century.

Etienne Gilson, the distinguished historian of philosophy, in the first semester of the academic year 1936–37 delivered the William James lectures at Harvard University, lectures that were eventually published under the title, *The Unity of Philosophical Experience*. Gilson based his lectures on the premise: "The history of philosophy is much more a part of philosophy itself than the history of science is part of science, for it is not impossible to become a competent scientist without knowing anything about the history of science, but no man can carry far his own philosophical reflections unless he first studies the history of philosophy."[1] Gilson was convinced that unless it can be shown that philosophy exhibits some intrinsic intelligibility, we have only an end-

less chain of mutually destructive systems that run from Thales to Karl
Marx.

Gilson wrote more than three quarters of a century ago. If one
examines what passes as academic philosophy today, one is likely to
doubt that there is any unity to philosophical experience. Much contemporary philosophy has little to do with the pursuit of wisdom, and
much is written without any knowledge of the history of philosophy.
Thus we can find a professor of moral philosophy, by his own admis-
sion, lecturing without any knowledge of the Stoics and another lecturer from a prominent university, in a nationally televised series of lectures, jumping, in a supposedly historical review, from Plato to
Descartes with nothing in between. Universities, intellectually democ-
ratized, have become centers for job certification. It is not just because
books and essays are generated in pursuit of appointment and tenure.
That is a fact, to be sure, but philosophy has become so specialized and
the language in which it is written so insular that it has little to offer
outside of more-or-less cloistered communities, be they Oxford,
Cambridge, or Columbia University. Contemporary philosophy rarely
speaks to lay interests, and when it does, it usually comes loaded with
an ideological bias.

"The main stream," as the term is employed here, is represented by
Plato, Aristotle, and St. Thomas, whom Gilson has called, "the three
greatest metaphysicians who ever existed," and by their commentators
through the ages. With Gilson, it must be noted: "Their ambition was
not to achieve philosophy once and for all, but to maintain it and to
serve it in their own time."[2] The main stream is carried within little
"communities of character," as Russell Kirk liked to call them, where
the legacy of Plato, Aristotle, and Aquinas is cultivated, albeit within a
fading Christian culture.

These essays and the accompanying reviews of recent Islamic
scholarship and works in the history of science are intended to bring to
life a time-tested perspective on their respective subjects. Part I is a collection of essays that address a number of contemporary social and
political issues. Part II consists of reviews of significant works in the
history of science which the author has published over the past decade
in the *Review of Metaphysics*. These show clearly that progress in sci-

ence had nothing to do with the abandonment of the Aristotelian or Scholastic tradition of philosophy as is often claimed by its adversaries. Part III is an introduction to Islamic scholarship that will aid those seeking an understanding of the origins and history of that movement.. All three sections of the book show the importance of history for an informed judgment on the course of contemporary events.

Part I – Essays

The Loss of Maritain's America

"Schrager Makes Over a Legendary Chicago Hotel" is the headline the *New York Times* gave to its report on the downscaling of Chicago's Ambassador East Hotel. The Ambassador East Hotel opened in 1924 on what is known as Chicago's Gold Coast. I can't say I know it well. My father, a Chicago hotelier, took me there as a child as part of a tour of the public spaces of some of Chicago's great hotels. The Ambassador East is known for its famous dining room, the Pump Room, as well as for the famous who dined there. Now, a few generations after its opening, the Ambassador East is being renovated, downgraded under a new name, the Public. Why? In the words of its owner, Ian Schrager, "The idea is to have a less expensive hotel . . . because I think the country is more complicated now. It is not going to be so much about upward mobility in the future."[1] A frightening prospect! This contrasts sharply with the America described by the French philosopher, Jacques Maritain, in his 1958 *Reflections on America*. A different country to be sure! On both sides of the Atlantic, one hears the refrain, "This is not the country I was born into." There is a pertinent scholastic axiom that goes something like this: an entity must preserve its identity if it is to preserve its very being.

As Prime Minister Nicholas Sarkozy currently grapples with the issue of French identity, one is drawn to that earlier work of Jacques Maritain, who attempted to take the measure, not of France but of America in a similarly troubled time. In *Reflections on America*, Maritain, in the spirit of Tocqueville, attempted to capture the American temperament as distinct from that of his native France, indeed, as distinct from that of Europe as a whole. Maritain was lecturing in North America when World War II broke out, and he remained in the United States throughout the war. His *Reflections* may be read as a love letter to America, as an expression of gratitude to his host country and to the people he came to appreciate. Sadly, the America described by Maritain in his 1958 assessment no longer exists. Some may say that, given Maritain's romantic account, it never existed.[2]

Maritain characterizes the American spirit as "one grounded in a sense of community, not in a set of abstract slogans or lofty ideals." He viewed the country as "a swarming multiplicity of particular communities, self-organized groups, associations, unions, sodalities, vocational and religious brotherhoods, in which men join forces with one another at the elementary level of their everyday concerns and interests."[3] In that light he could praise Martin Luther King for his Southern leadership and Saul Alinsky as a community organizer. With the principle of subsidiarity in mind, he saw in the "organic multiplicity" of these self-generated independent communities not only efficiency but a check on the power of the federal state.

Maritain found America to be a classless society in spite of an obvious disparity of income between rich and poor. The common man, in his experience, was neither servile nor arrogant. Maritain praised the ability of the country to integrate newcomers into the larger society, immigrants who entered the country by virtue of their own free choice. Recognizing that the country was comprised of men of different spiritual lineages, he nevertheless spoke of the United States as a religious commonwealth. He was appreciative of the insight of Will Herberg, a Jewish sociologist, who was writing at the time.[4] Herberg is remembered for his dictum, "To be an American is to be religious, and to be religious is to be religious in one of three ways, as a Protestant, Catholic or Jew." Maritain, himself, singled out the Jews for playing an essential and indispensable role in the dynamic ferment of American life.

Maritain acknowledged a growing trend toward secularism but hoped for an intelligent cooperation between Church and state. He feared a "temporalized religious inspiration" that could over time become institutionalized in the civic structures themselves, so much so that it would lose its essential supernatural character. With his friend, Barbara Ward, he believed that a recovery of faith in God is a necessary condition of Western freedom.[5] "There is," he wrote, "a possibility that in the course of centuries, America may become *embourgeoisée* — a nation interested only in its own material welfare and power." Having said that he adds, "The realization of such a possibility is, to my mind, improbable." He concludes his tribute with, "The great and admirable strength of America consists in this, that America is truly the American people."

Today, sixty-five years later, any reflective person is apt to notice the difference between Maritain's America and that of the present. A largely uneducated public has instantiated an anti-Christian, socialist regime at the federal level. A number of states now prevent the display of the Ten Commandments in classrooms and in the halls of the judiciary. Saul Alinsky's community initiative, perhaps never fully understood by Maritain, has been used to achieve ends Maritain never envisaged. Martin Luther King's laudable movement inspired Lyndon Johnson's affirmative action legislation with disastrous effects that are now acknowledged. The American character which Maritain lauded has been subverted by a flawed immigration policy and by the anti-Christian, intellectual elite's embrace of what we know as "multiculturalism" and "globalization." The public influence of Christianity has been muted. The once strong Catholic institutions of higher education are barely distinguishable from their state-supported counterparts. Religion has become so identified with almsgiving that Sunday worship seems at times merely a backdrop for yet another charitable appeal.

Two years after the appearance of Maritain's reflections, Friedrich A. von Hayek, published a major work, *The Constitution of Liberty*.[6] The Austrian economist was then a member of the Committee on Social Thought at the University of Chicago. Writing as an economist, he saw some things more clearly than Maritain and indeed was more pessimistic than Maritain about the future of the United States. In an earlier work, *The Road to Serfdom*,[7] Hayek, alarmed by the socialist drift on both sides of the Atlantic, issued what amounted to "a prophetic warning." From the perspective of von Hayek one could well predict Schrager's need to downsize the Ambassador East. Von Hayek saw clearly the ruinous economic effects that the nation's drift to socialism would likely bring. Not only that, he could show from the experience of Europe that the egalitarian impulse inevitably leads to coercion and a loss of personal freedom. In both England and the America of that day he found the same intellectual currents that facilitated the rise to power of Hitler, Mussolini, and Stalin. "When one hears for a second time," he wrote in 1944, "opinions expressed and measures advocated which one has met twenty years ago, they assume new meaning as symptoms

of a definite trend: they suggest that future developments will take a
similar turn." He continues, "It is necessary now to state the unpalatable truth that it is Germany whose fate we are now in danger of repeating." "The danger is not immediate," he wrote, "and conditions in
England and the United States are still so remote from those we have
witnessed in Germany as to make it difficult to believe that we are moving in the same direction."[8] Still he believed that the socialist policies
endorsed by "our progressive intellectuals" are the same as those of the
twenties and thirties that created National Socialism.

In *The Constitution of Liberty*, Hayek speaks to the nature of freedom and its defense, and of the many ways that freedom can be subverted, notably by inattention to the rule of law and, in the United
States, by inattention to the nation's founding documents. Without
employing the scholastic language of Maritain, he found the roots of
socialism in the positivist's denial that there is such a recognizable entity as human nature and a denial that positive, or manmade law, is
accountable to a higher law. Socialism in Hayek's view is based on an
ideology in direct opposition to a tradition which for two thousand
years has provided a conception of a law that is not manmade but found
in nature. He notes that in the 1930s, legal positivism had so conquered
Germany that "to be found guilty of adherence to natural-law theories
was a kind of social disgrace." He adds, "The possibilities which the
state of opinion created for an unlimited dictatorship were already seen
by acute observers at the time Hitler was trying to gain power."[9]

Among the gravest threats to freedom that Hayek identifies are the
regulatory agencies created by government that are essentially removed
from the rule of law, insofar as they possess in one body, legislative,
executive, and judicial authority. Once an area of jurisdiction has been
marked out for an agency by legislative or other authority, the agency
can act without exterior constraint. "Every public officer can act freely
according to his own discretion, and the courts will respect his action
as final and not inquire into its rightfulness."[10] The only issue any court
is likely to recognize is one of jurisdiction. Given the expansion of
government, one can find daily, by merely scanning the headlines,
examples of a drama being played out between regulatory agencies and
special interest groups, without regard for communal benefit. In the

final analysis the issue which divides is the nature of the *good* and how it is to be determined. Like Maritain, Hayek expressed in 1960 the hope that there still exists in the West wide consent on certain fundamental values. "Though I still regard myself as mainly an economist, I have come to feel more and more that the answers to many of the primary social questions of our time are ultimately to be found in the recognition of principles that lie outside the scope of technical economics or of any single discipline."[11] In a kind of lament, he notes, "A large part of the peoples of the world borrowed from Western civilization and adopted Western ideals at a time when the West became unsure of itself and lost faith in the traditions that have made it what it is."[12]

What Hayek intimates time and again from a purely secular perspective, Pope Benedict XVI has been saying explicitly. The West needs to recover a sense of the sacred. Benedict, cognizant of the declining influence of Christianity within the West, has in multiple addresses called attention to the role that Christianity has played in shaping Western culture, indeed, in unifying Europe. He has repeatedly called for an intellectual revival that recognizes the Church's past role and its continuing necessity as a unifying element to a divided Europe.[13] As Hayek acknowledged without explicitly saying so, it is the Church which has carried the intellectual mainstream through the ages and against which the questionable canons of our contemporary intelligentsia are to be measured.

Maritain in the Company of His Peers

It is well known that Robert M. Hutchins, as president of the University of Chicago, three times attempted to have Maritain appointed to the faculty of philosophy. The faculty at that time was headed by James Hayden Tufts. Three times Maritain was rejected on various grounds, once because he was proclaimed to be "an apologist." On another occasion he was rejected because he was thought to be "not a good philosopher." Hutchins shot back, "Do you have a good philosopher?" The answer, "No, but we will recognize one when we see one." He was similarly regarded by contemporaries such as Sidney Hook of New York University and Ernest Nagel of Columbia University, both of whom dismissed him with a derogatory remark in one forum or another. One must admit that there is ample ground for regarding him as an apologist. Maritain worked as a philosopher, but he worked within the context of the Catholic faith, devoting much of his work to issues that affected the faith in one way or another.

In an often neglected work, *The Degrees of Knowledge*, a treatise on the nature of scientific explanation, Maritain discusses divine grace, specifically the Western world's abuse of divine grace. In that work, he speaks of the Gifts of the Holy Spirit and of the rationalist's flight from God as metaphysical suicide. Drawing upon Hilaire Belloc's famous dictum, "Europe is the Faith, the Faith is Europe," Maritain writes, "If Hilaire Belloc means that Europe would be nothing without the faith and that its very reason for being has been and still is, to dispense faith to the world, he is right in saying Europe is the faith. But absolutely speaking, No, Europe is not the faith and the faith is not Europe. Rome is not the capital of the world. *Urbis caput orbis*. The Church is universal because it is born of God. All nations are at home in it."[1] He speaks of St. Thomas in a similar vein, suggesting that Thomas is a gift to the whole world by medieval Christianity "who belongs to neither one continent, nor to one century, whose doctrines are as universal as the Church is universal." All true enough, but one does not expect such remarks in a treatise on the nature of science. Ernest Nagel, whom I just mentioned, was the author of the most widely used textbook in the philosophy of science in the mid-decades of the twentieth century and the author of a work entitled, *Sovereign Reason*.[2] From Nagel's vantage point as a naturalist, or rationalist, Maritain could rightly be seen as an apologist, and indeed he was. Mortimer Adler, speaking of *The Degrees*, offered this defense: "I discern in it," he wrote, "the outlines, at least, of a synthesis of science, philosophy and theology which will do for us what St. Thomas did for philosophy and theology in the Middle Ages. . . . Maritain seems to me to be the only contemporary philosopher who has deeply sensed the movement of history, and the point at which we stand."[3]

On the positive side Etienne Gilson, while a prisoner of war in Germany, acquired a respect for Maritain from having read two articles by him. Maritain had found a home in the Institut Catholique de Paris that attracted scholars who, like Maritain, wanted to work as Catholics within the Aristotelian and scholastic traditions. Within the institute, professors were free to address such topics as the existence of God, teleology in nature, free will, and moral obligation as a basis of faith, issues which received scant attention in the state universities of the time. Maritain's work came to the attention of the French bishops who, in their effort to restore Catholic higher education, commissioned Maritain to prepare a series of college-level textbooks for use in the seminaries. Of a projected seven volumes, he completed two. His *Formal Logic* was subsequently translated into Italian and used as a seminary textbook by Giovanni Montini, later Paul VI. While working in the Vatican, Msgr. Montini also translated into Italian Maritain's *Three Reformers; Luther, Descartes and Rousseau*. As Pope, he quoted Maritain's work in his encyclical, *Populorum Progresso*, and later, at the end of Vatican II, it was to Maritain that he delivered his papal message to the intellectuals and scientists of the world. At the end of the ceremony, the Pope embraced the aging philosopher in the front of the crowd at St. Peter's Square.

But I am getting ahead of myself. Leo XIII on becoming Pope in 1878 was quick to endorse a fledgling Thomistic movement with his encyclical, *Aeterni Patris* (1879). Maritain contributed significantly to the movement. It was under Leo's patronage that the Institut Superior de Philosophie at Louvain opened in 1893 and the School of Philosophy at The Catholic University of America in 1889. Simon Depoloige, as president of the Institut Superior, in 1911 published a critique of Lucien Levy-Bruhl's *La morale et les science des moeurs*. Well received in Catholic circles, the book immediately enjoyed a second printing, and after the war was deemed worthy of a third printing (1923) in a series edited by Maritain, much to the chagrin of Etienne Gilson who early on had approvingly called it "an incredible book." Gilson by that time had become a professor at the Sorbonne, and Lucien Levy-Bruhl was a colleague. From that fortress, Gilson kept a polite distance from the neoscholastics at the Institut Catholique de Paris. As a professor within the University of Paris, Gilson worked primarily as an historian of philosophy, somewhat detached from the polemics of his co-religionists. He was not yet the Thomist of *Being and Some Philosophers*.

Maritain, it may be noted, had passed his *agrégation* in 1905 and was entitled to teach in one of the state lycees, but he decided to remain independent of any state affiliation, much to the satisfaction of his friend Ernest Psichari. Given his independence, Maritain proved to be a harsh critic of the prevailing philosophy of his day, the positivism of Comte and the Vienna Circle; he even wrote an unkind critique of the philosophy of his mentor, Henri Bergson. *Three Reformers* was an unmerciful attack on its subjects. But Nicholas Berdyaev in his autobiography had this to say in defense of Maritain, "When he wrote about the opponents of Roman Catholicism or of Thomism, he was harsh and caustic, but in reality he was extremely gentle, urbane, and generous and possessed a remarkable poise of mind and character. Maritain instantly won my heart. There was something irresistibly attractive for me even in his appearance."[4] Raïssa would say the same of Jacques, all tooth and claw in attacking doctrine in the abstract but kindly in dealing with the persons who actually held those doctrines.

T. S. Eliot once called Maritain, "the most conspicuous of figures and probably the most powerful force in contemporary philosophy." That may have been an exaggeration, but the wide-ranging interests of the Maritains in the arts and sciences attracted a wide circle of friends:

philosophers, theologians, painters, and poets who would gather at the Maritain home on a Sunday afternoon. Among them were Garrigou-Lagrange, Jean Cocteau, Etienne Gilson, Ernest Psichari, Nicholas Berdyaev, Emmanuel Mounier, François Mauriac, Marc Chagall, and Georges Rouault. Edith Stein was an occasional participant. Eliot in his celebrated Cambridge lecture, subsequently published as *The Idea of a Christian Society*,[5] acknowledged a debt to Maritain as well as to Christopher Dawson. They had no doubt written to each other for Maritain corresponded widely. Among those correspondents was Thomas Merton, who showed me some letters that Maritain had written shortly after the death of his beloved Raïssa. Merton found them unintelligible and so did I, not the least because of my limited French. I don't know what to make of a comment by the Protestant theologian, Reinhold Niebuhr, "Maritain possessed a quality of character that one would define as saintly, if that word had not such various connotations."[6]

I could continue in this vein indefinitely for Maritain touched the lives of many, pupils and colleagues to be sure, and countless others through his numerous books. We will give Yves Simon, who studied under Maritain at the Institut Catholique in the 1920s, the last tribute. He said of his professor, "Maritain's books bear the decisive characteristics of Great Books which is inexhaustibility. There is no end to the teaching you can draw from a Great Book. That is what we realize every time we read a book of Maritain."[7] The same could be said of Simon's own works.

I now turn to the unfavorable reception by his co-religionists of Maritain's last complete book, *De l'Église du Christ*, a work published in English translation in the year of his death.[8] It was ignored by the secular media and given scant notice in the Catholic press. It followed by seven years the publication of *Le Paysan de la Garonne*,[9] which had earned Maritain the enmity of the Catholic left for its critique of some of the theology developing in the wake of Vatican II. John Courtney Murray in *We Hold These Truths* (1960) noted happily that the Church in North America was not divided between left and right as it was with destructive consequences in Europe. By the close of Vatican II, the European virus had spread to North America. Maritain, who had been the darling of the liberal Catholic intelligentsia because of his social philosophy, was suddenly ostracized, his later works ignored. For Maritain a liberal social policy did not presuppose a liberal Catholic theology, certainly not one at war with the intellectual heritage of the Church.

In none of his critical studies does Maritain present himself as a theologian. He writes as a Catholic layman, as a philosopher, noticing the ambiguities, inconsistencies, and repudiations of key elements of the Catholic faith by prominent and influential theologians, who still called themselves somewhat dubiously "Catholic." No stranger to debate, Maritain challenged deviant positions with his customary acuity but without much success. Hardly surprising; the left characteristically avoids debate, preferring to ignore or ridicule its critics, which it easily does with the aid of a willing secular media. In the case of Maritain, he was simply ignored although one can find snide comments in the writings of a number of Catholic authors.

Maritain's ill treatment aside, his work proved to be prescient in a number of ways. John Paul II's *Fides et Ratio* and Benedict's *Dominus Iesus* carry elements of the debate, emphasizing the importance of philosophy to theology and the tendency of the ecumenical dialogue to blur irreconcilable differences in the interest of accommodation.

In *de l'Église du Christ* Maritain speaks of the "profoundly troubled historical moment" at which he was writing. Recognizing the need for an ecumenical outreach, he nevertheless decries the search for a spurious universalism whose first condition seems to be indifference with respect to truth. It is foolish, he holds, to attempt to unite all Christians in spite of their dissidences and all men in spite of the diversity of their beliefs. The great utopian ideal—unity of all Christians—can only be achieved with a complete disregard for the truth. One hears of "ecumenical dialogue" but not "ecumenical friendship." Is it not friendship, he asks, which is first required, well-established habits of friendship, created by fraternal banquets, eating, drinking, and smoking together, conversing at random, and joking? Such is far more useful than "the meetings of commissions with their definite programs, their reports, and their speeches. . . . The meal taken in common is a natural rite of human friendship."[10]

The subtitle of *On the Church of Christ: The Person of the Church and Her Personnel*, is indicative of a distinction that is crucial, Maritain believes, to an understanding of the Church. "Churchmen will never be the Church," he writes. One can take a detached view, making positive and negative assessments of the activity of Churchmen throughout the centuries while remaining confident of the holiness of the Church itself. This fundamental distinction runs throughout the book, the difference between the "person of the Church" and "her personnel," that is, between the Church visible to the intellect and the Church as visible to the eyes. "The person of the Church," writes Maritain, "can be holy while being composed of members who are all sinners to some degree."[11] Indeed, members who are holy can be guilty of gross error in their prudential judgments. Noble purposes can be pursued by ignoble means or frustrated by actions gone awry or by miscalculation and adverse circumstances.

That distinction made, Maritain defends the person of the Church while admitting the evils perpetrated in her name. No critic or cynic is likely to draw a longer list of the "sins of the Church," but those sins exist for the most part only in the popular mind, and it is surprising that Maritain took some of those alleged sins at face value. Serious scholarship in recent decades has challenged the popular take on most issues. Etienne Gilson, as a careful historian, would have been slow to apologize for sins of the Church that she or her Churchmen did not commit.

There is one area where Maritain forcefully comes to the defense of the Churchmen—namely, the treatment of the Jews. "The hatred of the Jewish people in the Middle Ages was the deed of the populace and of many in the bourgeoisie and in the nobility and many in the lower clergy. The high personnel of the Church, the Papacy above all, remained free from it."[12] He continues, "The Popes, even the ones most severe in their legislation, never knew this hatred."[13] It was in the papal states that the Jews fared best. "During the whole of the Middle Ages and the darkest periods of the latter, it was the Popes who were their greatest protectors and defenders."[14]

Maritain recognized that he was writing in "the midst of a tempest of widely diffused foolish ideas"[15] and that much of what he says will displease many. Yet he hoped that however poorly he has said it, in fifty

years' time the judgment may be made that "after all, it was not so stu-
pid." In fact, Maritain could be read as a preamble to Benedict's declaration, *Dominus Iesus,*[16] which calls to mind certain indispensable elements of Christian doctrine by providing a clear description of the
nature of the Church and its mission. The document proclaims, "God
has willed that the Church founded by Him be the instrument for the
salvation of *all* humanity . . . . This truth does not lessen the sincere
respect which the Church has for the religions of the world."[17] Yet the
fullness of Christianity, Benedict insists, is to be found only within the
Church, in Christ Himself who is "the way, the truth, and the life."

One is tempted to compare the work of Jacques Maritain with that
of Vladimir Soloviev (1853–1900).[18] While Maritain makes an important distinction between the Church and her personnel, Soloviev
advances a similar distinction between the Church of Rome and the
Latin Church, that is, between the functions of the Pope as Bishop of
Rome and as Patriarch of the West. "It is the Church of Rome, not the
Latin Church, that is the *mater et magistra omnium Ecclesiarum:* it is
the Bishop of Rome, and not the Western Patriarch, who speaks infal-
libly *ex cathedra.*" And Soloviev adds, "We ought not to forget that
there was a time when the Bishops of Rome were Greeks.[19] One could
find additional parallels between the thought of Maritain and Soloviev,
especially on the role of religion in society, on law and morality, and on
the treatment of the Jews.[20] Two laymen, philosophers, united by the
Catholic faith and a common love for classical philosophy, especially
Aristotle, writing across the divide wrought by the Great Schism, contribute by virtue of their professional skills to a common understanding
of the Church, later taught magisterially in *Fides et Ratio* and *Dominus
Iesus.*

Treason of the Intellectuals

Do we dare call them "anarchists"— environmentalists, federal regulators, whimsical judges, and other officials who seem to have abandoned the rule of law, if not reason itself? Perhaps "traitor" would be the better word. An anarchist is, by definition, one who disregards the law, challenges the prevailing order, or, in the case of the intellectual, one who undermines the culture. He need not be a bomb-throwing terrorist. Julian Benda, in *La trahison des clercs*[1] makes the case that the most serious form of anarchy is the treason of the intellectuals. Benda uses the term *clerc* to designate, as a class, writers, men of learning, artists, moralists, and churchmen. They are by vocation the officiants of time-transcending standards relevant to their calling. They become traitors when, abandoning objectivity, they display a special affinity for the group with which they identify.

One does not have to reach far to find examples of the subjectivity condemned by Benda. It can be found in appeals for judicial diversity on both sides of the Atlantic. British Justice Kenneth Clarke has argued that ethnicity and gender should be taken into account in making judicial appointments. Apparently the British judiciary is predominantly white male. His opinion reflects the claim that a white male judge can see things only from a white male's point of view, whereas a Latino woman judge will make decisions that reflect her Latino woman's outlook. In the United States we find a sitting Supreme Court justice saying that judges who set aside their ethnicity "do a disservice to society and the law."[2] It is evident from Benda's point of view that those who demand judicial diversity have implicitly given up on the rule of law.

That a state of cultural and political disorder exists within both the European Union and the United States is widely acknowledged and hardly needs illustration. Western nations on both sides of the Atlantic are confronted by massive immigrations of alien peoples who refuse assimilation within their adopted country and who demand accommodation for the customs they bring. The host countries themselves find it difficult to agree with respect to what may be demanded of the new-comer. Confusion abounds even with respect to what constitutes the national identity that the newcomer is encouraged to adopt. No one has asserted this more clearly than Pierre Manent in his book, *Democracy without Nations: The Fate of Self-Government in Europe*.[3] Manent is convinced that Europe is on the verge of self-destruction. The demo-cratic nation, he fears, has been lost in Europe, the very first place it appeared. "The European Union's political contrivances," he writes, "have become more and more artificial. With each day they recede fur-ther from the natural desires and movements of their citizens' souls."[4] A nation, he holds, is the same people living in the same place, observ-ing the same customs, abiding by the same moral principles. In Manent's judgment, Europe's governing classes, without explicitly say-ing so, aspire to create a homogeneous and limitless human world. In fact, given its intellectual climate, what distinguishes Europeans from one another and others cannot be evaluated or even publicly discussed.

Jocelyn Maclure and Charles Taylor, both Canadians, in a recent work claim that "One of the most important challenges facing contemporary societies is how to manage moral and religious diversity."[5] Taylor and Maclure find that a broad consensus exists to the effect that "secularism is an essential component of any liberal democracy com-prised of citizens who adhere to a plurality of conceptions of the world and of the good, whether these conceptions be religious, spiritual, or sec-ular."[6] Secularism they define as "a political and legal system whose function is to establish a certain distance between the state and religion."[7] But as conceived by Taylor and Maclure, it is more than that. The state in their view must be neutral toward the multiple values, beliefs, and life plans of citizens within modern societies. The state must be the state of all citizens and not identify itself with one particular religion or world view. And yet, "A liberal and democratic society cannot remain indiffer-ent to certain core principles such as human dignity, basic human rights, and popular sovereignty."[8] Several questions are clearly begged. Whence the core principles? How can there be a democratic society unless there is a certain cultural unity among the people who presumably form it? The core principles alluded to are not universal or found in the culture of all who seek asylum in the West. Modern liberalism depends on something it did not create, on traditionally shared beliefs and moral principles. Absent the cohesion provided by tradition, states are forced to become more legalistic and coercive in order to maintain stability and security. Still, Taylor and Maclure insist: "In showing itself to be agnostic on questions of the aims of human existence, the secular state recognizes the sovereignty of the person in his or her choice of conscience."[9] This amounts to an invitation to civil discord, as like-minded individuals group for ascendancy. Even within a Muslim country, where Islam is proclaimed in common, Sunni and Shi'a vie for control.

A compelling response to Taylor and Maclure is to be found in a recent work by Marcello Pera, former president of the Italian Senate, now professor of political philosophy at the Pontifical Lateran University, Rome.[10] Pera takes the title of his book, *Why We Should Call Ourselves Christians*, from an essay by Benedetto Croce, a professed atheist who nevertheless said of *we Europeans,* "Why We Cannot but Call Ourselves Christian." Croce, in spite of his materialism, was convinced that the objective and transcendent formulation of man's dignity and freedom is to be found in Christianity. Pera is insistent: "We should call ourselves Christian if we want to maintain our liberties and preserve our civilization . . . . If, as Thomas Jefferson claimed, our liberties must have, or must be felt as if they had, a religious foundation in order to bind the union together, then today's secularized Europe, which rejects that foundation, can never be politically united."[11] Pera continues, "Unlike Americans, Europeans cannot adopt a constitution beginning with the words 'We the people' because 'the people' must exist as a moral and spiritual community before such a constitution could be conceived and asked for."[12] The version of the European Constitution that was finally adopted after being rejected in popular referendums by the French and the Dutch made no reference to God or to Christianity and amounted to no more than a treaty between nations.

In addressing the moral decline which he finds on both sides of the Atlantic, Pera writes: "Liberal civilization was born in defense of the negative liberties of man. When the positive liberties of citizens burgeoned forth, everything started changing. The liberal state first became democratic, next paternalistic, and finally entered the totalitarian phase of the dictatorship of the majority and the tyranny of absolute authorities. No aspect of life today, from cradle to the grave, has been left untouched by legislation, and most of all by the verdicts of judges or supreme courts, or by the decisions of supranational institutions."[13] He fears that within democracies decisional authority is today being handed over to powerful interest groups and bureaucracies. Good and evil in the absence of an authoritative moral tradition, Pera maintains, tend to be determined not by transcendent moral principles but by parliamentary vote.

How this state of affairs came to pass is the subject of Brad S. Gregory's remarkably erudite treatise, The Unintended Reformation.[14] Gregory finds that modernity is failing because of the naturalistic or materialistic assumptions that pervade the academic world. Reason alone in modern philosophy, he argues, has proven no more capable than "scripture alone" in devising persuasive answers to what he calls Life Questions. Modernity has produced no substantive common outlook but instead has produced an open-ended welter of arbitrary truth claims. Ever-expanding technological capacities afforded by scientific advance are set within an increasingly rancorous culture of moral disagreement, leaving political direction rudderless.

The failure of modern philosophy to provide convincing answers with respect to the important questions of life is in part due to the exclusion from the academy of alternative religious and metaphysical world views. Fruitful dialogue is rendered impossible in spite of the fact, as Gregory points out, that: "Intellectually sophisticated expressions of religious world views exist today within Western hyperpluralism," but those views have been banished from secular research universities.[15] Theology, the philosophy of God, or what Aristotle called "divine science," and non-skeptical biblical scholarship find no place in the secular academy. As a consequence, most scholars and scientists are notably lacking in theological sophistication and even self-awareness of their own metaphysical assumptions and beliefs. Gregory is not optimistic that change is likely in the near future. "Unsecularizing the academy," he writes, " would require, of course, an intellectual openness on the part of scholars and scientists sufficient to end the long-standing modern charade in which naturalism has been assumed to be demonstrated, self-evident, ideologically neutral, or something arrived at on the basis of impartial inquiry."[16]

One gropes in vain for a happy prognosis. Could it be, in the words of Charles Murray, that "Europe's run is over"? Modern science arose first in Europe in a culture that alone made it possible. The technology based on that science is now universal, even as Europe in the twentieth century lost faith in its inherited culture. One could say, in the language of Benda, that it has been betrayed by its clerks, who, ignoring the classical and Christian sources of its greatness have left Europe little to defend but its material accomplishments. Many of its institutions are now governed by those who have not contributed to, and who do not share, the cultural outlook of what used to be called "Christendom." Julian Benda in his day called for a cosmopolitan Europe, indeed for a kind of globalization, based on a renewed respect for the things of spirit and a commitment to the objective and to the rational. Perhaps, in the words of Benda, "a handful of men at desks may be able to succeed in making humanity believe that the supreme values are the things of spirit."[17] Benedict XVI on almost a daily basis calls for Europe to awaken to its endangered heritage, but his is a voice crying in the wilderness.

Two Treatises on the Acquisition and Use of Power

Some cultural historian of the future, some future Gibbon will record the decline and fall of a once great nation, how it lost contact with its founding documents and with the spiritual traditions which animated its growth and how it succumbed to the siren song of a charismatic leader who led it to its dissolution in a visionary, multicultural, universal democracy.

As the United States in a troubled time faces a questionable future, we instinctively turn to the past to determine in the light of similar circumstances what the future may portend. To the untutored eye, studies of the past with reference to the future, although always an active literary genre, seem to be appearing with greater frequency. Rémi Brague has employed his significant command of medieval history to explore the relation that prevailed among Christianity, Islam, and Judaism in the Middle Ages, with an eye on the current European effort to integrate an Islamic influx from the Middle East and North Africa.[1] Adrian Goldsworthy has produced a new study of the decline and fall of the Roman Empire, and though he disclaims any thought of relevance to the present, he cannot avoid reference to the United States and even cites his participation in a seminar of established historians organized by the Center for Strategic and Budgetary Assessment under United States sponsorship. After chronicling the course of the Roman Empire from its peak at the death of Marcus Aurelius in 180 to the abortive effort of the Eastern Empire to recapture its lost territories in the sixth century, Goldsworthy, in his conclusion, assures the reader that the United States is not of necessity destined to repeat the Roman decline.[2] Paul A. Rahe has produced a study of Montesquieu on war, religion, and commerce that he clearly regards as relevant to contemporary political discourse.[3]

Apart from these serious studies, two treatises on the use and acquisition of power written in the mid-decades of the twentieth century are worth revisiting, for they retain a frightful puissance. I have in mind those of Bertrand de Jouvenal and F. A. Hayek.

I

Though often neglected as a cultural historian, Bertrand de Jouvenal's work, *On Power: Its Nature and the History of Its Growth*,[4] remains timely although it was written more than sixty years ago. Penned during the dark days of the Nazi occupation of France, the book was published at first opportunity in 1945 and appeared in English translation five years later. Up against the raw power of the German occupation, de Jouvenal, the philosopher and historian, was led to reflect on the nature of power in the abstract. He set out to examine the reasons why and the way in which Power grows in society. As he uses the word, "Power" is always capitalized; it may stand for authority, the ruler, or simply the drive for dominance.

On Power can be read at different levels: as history, as prophecy, as political theory. Pierre Manent, exploring the course of self-government in Europe, speaks of de Jouvenal's "melancholy liberalism."[5] Given de Jouvenal's sweeping command of history, he can make a case for every judgment or argument he advances in the book by citing numerous historical examples in support, yet his experience of Hitler's rise to power in the 1930s cannot be discounted as a coloring factor. The book is a call for repeated stock-taking, for an extended scrutiny of every new proposal that would extend the power of the state. Do not leap into the dark, he cautions his countrymen at war's end; beware of letting "necessity," the tyrant's plea, have its way.

Politics are about Power, he tells us. "It is in the pursuit of Utopia that the aggrandizers of state power find their most effective ally. Only an immensely powerful apparatus can do all that the preachers of panacea government promise."[6] De Jouvenal believes that history shows that the acceptance of all-embracing state authority is largely due to the fatigue and despair brought about by war or economic disorder. The European may say that liberty is the most precious of all things, yet as the experience of France attests, it is not valued as such by people who lack bread and water. The will to be free in time of danger is easily extinguished. Liberty becomes a secondary need; the primary need is security.

One of the pitfalls of democracy is its lack of accountability. The popular will is easily manipulated. It recognizes no authority outside itself that possesses the strength to limit its excesses. The dethronement of the old faith to which the state was accountable left an aching void in the domain of beliefs and principles, allowing the state to impose its own. Without accountability, democracy because of its centralizing, pattern-making, absolutist drive, can easily become an incubator of tyranny. The kings of old, the personification of power, were possessed of personality, possessed of passions good and bad. More often than not, their sense of responsibility led them to will "the good" for their people. Power within a democracy, by contrast, resides in a faceless and impersonal bureaucracy that claims to have no existence of its own and becomes the anonymous, impersonal, passionless instrument of what is presumed to be the general will. Writing in France when the Roosevelt administration was barely ten years old, de Jouvenal feared the long-range danger posed by the many regulatory commissions created by that administration. He saw that agencies possessing at once legislative, executive, and judicial control could operate largely outside of public control and become tyrannical.

The extension of Power, which means its ability to control ever more completely a nation's economy, is responsible for its ability to wage war. De Jouvenal asks, "Had Hitler succeeded Maria Theresa on the throne, does anyone suppose that it would have been possible to forge so many up to date weapons of tyranny?"[7] It is alas no longer possible for us to believe that by smashing Hitler and his regime we are eradicating the root of statist evil.

> "Can anyone doubt that a state which binds man to itself by every tie of need will be better placed to conscript them all, and one day consign them to the dooms of war? The more departments of life that Power takes over, the greater will be its material resources for making war."[8] Even within a democracy the vast resources of the state are ripe for a dictator to seize. The bold, by discounting all risk, are positioned to seize all initiatives and become the rulers, while the timid run for cover and security. "The more complete the hold which the state gets on the resources of a nation, the higher, the more sudden, the more irresistible, will be the wave in which an armed community can break on a pacific one . . . . It follows

that, in the very act of handing more of ourselves to the state, we may be fostering tomorrow's war."[9]

Aristotle in the *Politics* reduced the variety of governmental structures that he had studied to three: monarchy, aristocracy, and democracy, recognizing that whatever shape a government takes, the essence of governing is Power. Force may establish Power, but once established, habit alone can keep it in being. A standing center of Power which is obeyed by habit has, in the case of the state, the means of physical compulsion and is kept in being partly by its perceived strength, partly by the faith that it rules by right, and partly by the hope of its beneficence. The natural tendency of Power is to grow. Power is authority, and authority enables the expansion of authority.[10]

Power, when dedicated to egalitarian pursuits, must always be at war with capitalist authorities and despoil the capitalists of their accumulated wealth.[11] Its political objective consists in the demolition of a class that enjoys "independent means," by seizing the assets of that class to bestow benefits on others. The result is a transfer of power from productive individuals to an unproductive bureaucracy that becomes the new ruling class, displacing that which was economically productive. The top state authorities, in alliance with the bottom (that is, the oppressed), squeeze out the middle (the Establishment) and in doing so progressively penetrate ever deeper into the personal lives of citizens. The point of course has been made by others, notably by F. A. Hayek, who called attention to the fact that an assault on property rights is not always apparent because it is carried out in the name of the common good, an appealing but elastic concept defined by those whose interest it serves.

Given that all political activity is concerned with the acquisition of Power, both to seize and to maintain the organs of Power, one must first gain control of public education at its early stages. A state monopoly in education has the ability to condition minds in childhood for its later years, thereby preparing popular opinion for the seizure by the state of even greater Power.[12] De Jouvenal reminds his reader that in times past Western Europe has acknowledged that there is a superior will to the collective will of man and that there is an immutable law to which even civil authority must bow. Absent that acknowledgment, Power has free reign. "Even the police regime, the most insupportable attribute of tyranny, has grown in the shadow of democracy."[13] France, disliking the minority rule of one person, deposed the crown and subsequently organized itself in the light of mass interests only to discover that when the majority holds Power over a minority, justice within a democracy can be as elusive as it is in a despotic regime.

De Jouvenal's translator couldn't resist a postscript, "One of the first casualties in times of discord is, as Thucydides noted, the meaning of words, and to the Thucydidean list of inexactitudes, it is time to add the current equation of liberty with security, the possession of a vote with liberty, and justice with equality . . . of democratic with whatever the user of the word happens to approve. Humpty Dumpty has succeeded to the chair of more precise thinkers."[14]

Yves R. Simon, a French contemporary of de Jouvenal, born in 1903, the same year as de Jouvenal, (Simon in Cherbourg, de Jouvenal in the Champagne region), and de Jouvenal were both in their early thirties when they witnessed Hitler's rise to power. At the outbreak of the war, Simon was a visiting professor in the United States. Remaining in America, he eventually became a member of the Committee on Social Thought at the University of Chicago. From this vantage point, Simon, like de Jouvenal, surveyed the ruins of Europe and in his own way addressed the conditions that brought it about.[15] Influenced by Pierre Joseph Proudhon, no friend of democracy, Simon was fearful that democracy, far from excluding a totalitarian regime, would in time actually give way to one. Absent appropriate checks and balances, the legal processes of the democratic state may work in such away as to allow the elimination of democracy. Of equal importance to whatever checks and balances may be prescribed by law or inscribed in a constitution, are those that are in a sense external to the political structure, namely, private property and independent management of resources. "When people acquiesce to the removal of all checks on the conquering expansion of the state, the totalitarian regime is firmly established." Simon was convinced that an impersonal authority could not win such an irrational surrender but that a leader with charismatic talents could win approval.[16] We know from experience, he says, that where totalitarianism prevails, democracy has no chance, yet few men dare to voice the paradoxical consideration that democracy may become totalitarian. Totalitarian democracy, of course, would not be true democracy.[17] Proudhon maintains that the state, whether democratic or not, remains the state and of its very nature threatens all liberties and the very life of society.

De Jouvenal has yet another concern. In a democratic regime, we are told, the general interest is represented by Power. From this postulate flows the corollary that no interest is legitimate that opposes the general interest. For this reason even local or particular interest must yield to the general interest, in de Jouvenal's words, "bend its knee to Power." Power, which is conceived as the incarnation of the general wish, cannot tolerate any group which embodies less general wishes and interests.[18]

The distinguished American historian, Richard Pipes, a former director of Harvard's Russian Research Center and a specialist in Russian history, reinforces de Jouvenal's judgment that democratic procedures in electing government officials do not guarantee respect for individual rights. The right to property, he holds in his book entitled, *Property and Freedom*,[19] may be more important than the right to vote. Property of itself does not guarantee civil rights and liberties, but, historically speaking, it has been the most effective device for ensuring both. Property has the effect of creating an autonomous sphere on which, by mutual consent, neither the state nor society can encroach. In drawing a line between the public and the private sphere, it makes its owner, as it were, co-sovereign with the state.

Even so, once "the elimination of poverty" becomes a state objective, the state is bound to treat property not as a fundamental right that it has an obligation to protect but as an obstacle to "social justice."[20] Even in the most advanced democracies, the main threat to liberty may come not from tyranny but from the pursuit of socialist objectives. Liberty by its very nature, Pipes reminds us, is inegalitarian. Men differ in strength, intelligence, ambition, courage, perseverance, and all else that makes for success. There is no method to make men both free and equal. In the pursuit of equality, property rights may be subtly undermined through taxation and government interference with business contracts as the state pursues its egalitarian objectives. Insofar as poor voters always and everywhere outnumber rich ones, in theory there are no limits to the democratic state's drive to promote equality and to run roughshod over the rights of private property. "The rights to ownership,"[21] Pipes argues, "need to be restored to their proper place instead of being sacrificed to the unattainable ideal of social equality and all embracing economic security. . . . The balance between 'civil' and 'property' rights has to be readdressed if we care about freedom." He continues, "The Civil Rights Act of 1964 gave the government no license to set quotas for hiring personnel by private enterprise or admitting students to institutions of higher learning, and yet the federal bureaucracy acts as if it had."[22] Some fear, Pipes acknowledges, that some believe that the drive for social justice will inevitably lead to the destruction of democracy, yet he is not drawn to that pessimistic conclusion. He reasons that encroachments on property cannot advance relentlessly to their logical conclusion, the abolition of private property, because the most affluent are twice as likely to vote as the weakest. If he were addressing the subject today, some ten years later, I am not sure he would be so sanguine. The prospect of government control of all aspects of the electoral process looms as the present administration is now positioned to mobilize the vote through federally funded organizations and through redistricting by taking direct control of the census. Not to be discounted is the distorting effect of a monolithic media able to advance its own political agenda in concert with officials who share its objectives. De Jouvenal addressed this issue when speaking of the ability of popular newspapers to awaken emotion, building or destroying concepts of right conduct. "From the day the first ha'penny paper was launched until now, the big circulation newspapers have never built up an ethic."[23]

In concluding paragraphs of his study, de Jouvenal writes, "It is impossible to condemn totalitarian regimes without also condemning the destructive metaphysics which made their happening a certainty."[24] He asks, "What would the individualists and free thinkers of the eighteenth and nineteenth centuries say could they but see what idols a man must now worship, to what jackboot he must now pay homage; would not the superstition they fought seem to be the very acme of enlightenment, compared to the superstitions which have taken its place?"[25] It is with reason that Pierre Manent called him a "melancholy liberal."

II

It was approximately sixty-five years ago that the Austrian economist, F. A. Hayek (1899–1992), published a short work entitled *The Road to Serfdom,* a book perhaps more relevant today than when it was written.[26] The book is the result of Hayek's reflection on the socialist drift in Europe that facilitated the rise to power of Hitler, Mussolini, and Stalin. When the Anschluss Osterreichs took place in March 1938, Hayek was a lecturer at the London School of Economics. Granted British citizenship, he remained throughout the war years in England, where he continued to teach until 1950 when he accepted an appointment to the Committee on Social Thought at the University of Chicago.

Written while the outcome of World War II was still uncertain, *The Road to Serfdom* may be fruitfully read as an historical review of the social and economic policies that prevailed during the first decades of the twentieth century, but that was not Hayek's primary purpose in writing the book. It was issued as a prophetic warning, yet as Hayek modestly writes, one does not need to be a prophet to be aware of impending disaster. "When one hears for the second time opinions expressed and measures advocated which one has met twenty years ago, they assume a new meaning as symptoms of a definite trend: they suggest the probability that future developments will take a similar turn."[27] He continues, "It is necessary now to state the unpalatable truth that it is Germany whose fate we are now in danger of repeating. The danger is not immediate, it is true, and conditions in England and the United States are still so remote from those we have witnessed in Germany as to make it difficult to believe we are moving in the same direction." Still, he complains, the socialist policies endorsed by our "progressive" intellectuals are the same as those of the twenties and thirties that created National Socialism.

Hayek was not alone in his analysis of the past or in recognizing the danger that the emerging socialist parties posed for the future of Europe. As we have seen, Bertrand de Jouvenal, writing in France during the same period, produced a similar diagnosis of the events that brought the European dictators to power. De Jouvenal's study of power and its acquisition serves as a lasting reminder that politics is about power. "It is in the pursuit of Utopia," de Jouvenal writes, "that the aggrandizers of state power find their most effective ally, [for] only an immensely powerful apparatus can do all that the preachers of panacea government promise." Hayek, much more than de Jouvenal, was engaged in a debate on economic planning that included Ludwig von Mises, a pupil of Eugen Böhm-Bawerk, Joseph Schumpeter, Michael Polanyi, Otto Neurath, Walter Schiff, and Karl Popper.

It is significant that the debate in which Hayek was engaged focused not so much on social policy per se as it did on the method to be employed in systematically arriving at sustainable social policy. The remarkable advances in the natural sciences in the late nineteenth and early twentieth centuries, particularly in theoretical physics, stimulated interest in methodological and epistemological issues normally discussed in the philosophy of science. The positivism of the Vienna Circle did not remain merely a philosophical outlook but began to have an impact in the social sciences.[28] The methods which had proven successful in natural science were deemed applicable to the sciences of man. Economics was no exception. Positivism, eschewing the metaphysical concepts of nature and purpose in nature, limited knowledge to sense experience, to that which can be empirically verified, thereby reducing science to description and prediction. Lost was a sense of an unchangeable human nature, ordered to a discernible end, that is, to self-fulfillment.

Positivism, given its ideological link to socialism, tended to divide political theorists into left and right. Perhaps no one has more succinctly shown the link than the American political theorist, John H. Hallowell, in his *Main Currents in Modern Political Thought*.[29] This should be read in conjunction with Ludwig von Mises's classic but lumbering 1922 volume, *Socialism: An Economic and Sociological Analysis*.[30] Hallowell shows that once justice, being a metaphysical concept, is discarded as empirically worthless, freedom under the law no longer means what the classical liberal took it to mean. Traditionally it meant that a man could not be compelled to do anything contrary to reason and conscience. Under the influence of positivism "freedom" came to mean that a man could not be compelled to do anything except by law enacted in accordance with some prescribed procedure with sufficient force behind it to compel obedience. From the positivist's viewpoint what the liberal called "rights" are merely concessions granted by the state or society. Hallowell concludes that if rights are the product of law, they are not properly rights at all; they are mere concessions to claims that the individual makes and the state recognizes. As such they can be withdrawn if the state deems such withdrawal is in the interest of the general welfare. "There is a great difference," Hallowell insists, "between freedom from unjust compulsion and freedom from illegal compulsion. Moreover, when the test of legality is ultimately conceived as the force behind law, freedom from illegal compulsion amounts to no more than freedom to do whatever the state does not forbid. This is a conception of freedom much more congenial to tyranny than to the preservation of the inalienable rights of man."[31] Viewed from the perspective of positivism, the rights of man are no longer to be called "natural rights:" they are mere "legal rights." Hallowell reflects: "It was the liberal positivistic jurist long before Hitler who taught (explicitly or implicitly) that might makes right and that rights are not attributes which individuals have by virtue of their humanity but simply claims which the state may or may not choose to recognize. Unwittingly, it may be, such liberals prepared the way for Lidice and Dachau."[32]

Distancing himself from socialist planning, Hayek provided his own perspective on how a market economy is actually driven. Most of the knowledge necessary for running an economic system, he holds, is not in the form of scientific knowledge, that is, by a conscious allusion to the principles governing natural and social phenomena. More important is the knowledge which may be described as intuitive in character, idiosyncratic knowledge, consisting of dispersed bits of information and understanding relative to time and place. This tacit knowledge is often not consciously possessed by those who make use of it, and it is of such a nature that it can never be communicated to a central authority. The market tends to use this tacit knowledge as do individuals pursuing their own ends.

Ludwig von Mises had made a similar point in a 1920 article entitled, "Economic Calculation in the Socialist Commonwealth," wherein
he wrote, "In the absence of a capitalist market, production costs and
commodity values could not be determined. A central planning board
could neither measure costs nor determine prices. Prices reflect not
inherent but changing human preferences; they provide producers and
distributors necessary information for planning production and distribution."[33] "It is," he continues, "precisely in market dealings that market
prices are formed, taken as the basis of calculation for all kinds of goods
and labor. Where there is no free market, there is no pricing mechanism:
without a pricing mechanism there is no economic calculation."[34]

Karl Popper, like Hayek, was a student of von Mises and from the
start was critical of the Vienna Circle, although in his early years he
could be described as a heterodox socialist. Hayek badly shook
Popper's progressivism, Hacohen tell us in his biography of Popper. On
reading *The Road to Serfdom,* Popper in a letter to Hayek, called it "one
of the most important political books I have ever seen."[35] To another
correspondent he wrote, "[Hayek] has seen very much sharper than I
have that socialism itself leads directly to totalitarianism."[36] Popper in
his autobiography discloses that he would have remained a socialist had
he not begun to see that socialism put liberty at risk. In Hacohen's judgment, it was the Continent's mass support for fascism that gave him
pause. Popper came to the conclusion that "the paradox of democracy
was real: if the majority was sovereign, then it could decide that it no
longer wished a democratic government. It could, as a third of the
German electorate did, vote the fascists to power."[37] It is worth remem-
bering that both Hayek and Karl Popper, though universally recognized
as social theorists, were initially interested in epistemological issues
normally encountered in the philosophy of science. In fact, when Hayek
arrived at the University of Chicago, he offered a faculty seminar of the
philosophy of science that was attended by some of the most notable
scientists of the time, including Enrico Fermi, Sewall Wright, and Leo
Szilard.

In *The Fatal Conceit,* Hayek devotes a timely chapter to the
"Mysterious World of Trade and Money," wherein he speaks of the
shameless abuse of money by governments and the disturbance in

markets caused by government interference. "The history of government management of money has, except for a few short happy periods, been one of incessant fraud and deception."[38] With von Mises he was a strong advocate of the gold standard. He was convinced that society does not benefit from an artificial increase in the money supply or the easy availability of bank credit. Credit expansion by banks, in addition to causing inflation, makes depression inevitable by causing malinvestment, that is, by inducing businessmen to overinvest in higher inventories of capital goods. Inflationary bank credit, when loaned to businesses, masquerades as pseudo-savings and makes businessmen believe that there are more resources available to invest in capital goods production than consumers genuinely command. Hence an inflationary boom requires a recession, which becomes a painful but necessary process by which the market liquidates unsound investments and reestablishes the investment and productive structure that best satisfies consumer preferences and demands. In the early 1920s von Mises and Hayek developed this cyclical theory, warning that the "New Era" prosperity of the period was a sham and that its inevitable result would be a bank panic and depression.[39] Contemporary readers may find it unfortunate that the von Mises-Hayek thesis has made no lasting impression on the U.S. administrations past and present.

Socialism, considered abstractly, Hayek concedes, may not inexorably lead to totalitarian rule, but he is convinced that experience shows that the unforeseen and inevitable consequences of social planning create a state of affairs in which, if its policies are pursued, totalitarian forces eventually will get the upper hand. Ironically, he suggests, socialism can be put into practice only by methods of which socialist disapprove.[40] *The Road to Serfdom* was written, Hayek repeats, in an effort to alert his readers to the seemingly unstoppable trend in Western democracies to subject their national economies to central planning, which he claims evidence shows will inevitably lead to tyranny. Even a strong tradition of political liberty, Hayek warns, is no safeguard. The democratic statesman who from the loftiest of motives sets out to plan economic life will soon be confronted with the alternative of assuming dictatorial power or abandoning his plans.[41] In short order he will have to choose between disregard of ordinary morals and failure. Hayek is convinced that the unscrupulous and uninhibited, lacking principles to constrain their activity, are most likely to assume positions of authority. Under their leadership, the moral views that initially inspired the collectivist state are not likely to prevail. The general demand for quick and determined government action will lead to a new morality and the suppression of democratic procedures. Given dissatisfaction with the slow and cumbersome course of constitutional procedures, the man or the party that appears the strongest and seems the most resolute in getting things done is the one that will set the moral tone.[42]

In a planned society it is not merely a question of what the majority of people agree upon but what the largest single or homogeneous group agrees upon. It takes such a core group to make unified direction possible.[43] Such a group, Hayek believes, is not likely to be formed by the best elements of society. In general the higher the education and intelligence of individuals, the more their tastes will differ and the less likely they are to agree on a set of ideas. "If we wish to find a high degree of uniformity and similarity of outlook, we have to descend to the regions of moral and intellectual standards where the more primitive and 'common' instincts and truths prevail."[44]

That said, if a political dictator had to rely entirely on those whose uncomplicated and primitive instincts happen to be similar, their numbers would scarcely give sufficient weight to his campaign. He will have to increase their numbers by converting more to the same creed.[45] He must somehow obtain support of the docile and gullible who have no strong convictions of their own but who are prepared to accept a ready-made system of values provided it is drummed into their ears loudly and frequently. It will be those whose vague and imperfectly formed ideas are easily swayed and whose passions and emotions are readily aroused who will thus swell the ranks of the totalitarian party.[46] Absent a strong bourgeoisie (middle class), the transition to a dictatorship may be easy, swift, and accomplished with complete legality.

Speaking of the mechanism by which power is achieved, Hayek warns that where there is dissatisfaction with the policies of the ruling party, a skillful demagogue can weld together a closely coherent and homogeneous body of supporters by calling for a new order. "It seems almost a law of human nature that it is easier to get people to agree on a negative program—on the hatred of an enemy, on the envy of those who are better off—than on any positive task."[47] Yet pandering to the demands of a minority can lead to the dissolution of democratic governance, for democratic governance can work successfully so long as, by a widely accepted creed, the functions of the state are limited to policies where real agreement among the majority can be achieved. The price we have to pay for a democratic system, Hayek insists, is the restriction of state action to those areas where agreement can be reached. Government interference in the life of the citizenry, even for benevolent purposes, endangers liberty if it posits a consensus where none exists. Absent consensus, coercion becomes necessary.[48]

Examining the wellsprings of the socialist mentality, Hayek believes that the desire to organize social life according to a unitary plan springs essentially from a desire for power, much more so than a desire for the communal good. In order to achieve their end, socialists must create power—power over men wielded by other men, a perennial allure regardless of the objective. The success of socialist planning will depend on the achievement of power over a reluctant citizenry. When economic power is employed as an instrument of political power, it creates a degree of dependence scarcely distinguishable from slavery. The separation of economic and political aims, Hayek insists, is an essential condition of freedom.[49]

Throughout his long life, Hayek was to return time and again to themes first articulated in *The Road to Serfdom,* notably in *Law, Legislation and Liberty*[50] and *The Fatal Conceit: The Errors of Socialism* (cited earlier). In the latter, published when Hayek was eighty-nine years old, he professed to be an agnostic with respect to the existence and nature of God, but he had no doubt about the classical and Christian origins of Western culture, and he saw that with the eclipse of Christianity, Europe was losing a force for the good. In this work the connection between property and liberty is reexamined in the light of history. "The Greco-Roman world," Hayek writes, "was essentially and precisely one of private ownership, whether of a few acres or of the enormous domains of Roman senators and emperors, a world of private trade and manufacture."[51] The Greeks seem to have been the first to see the connection between private property and individual freedom. From antiquity to the present, "no advanced civilization has yet developed without a government which saw its chief aim in the protection of private property."[52] "Where there is no property, there is no justice" is a proposition as certain as any demonstration in Euclid, Hayek maintains. Why then do intelligent people tend to be socialist? "Of course intelligent people," he responds, "will tend to overvalue intelligence, and to suppose that we must owe all the advantages and opportunities that our civilization offers to deliberate design rather than to following traditional rules, and likewise to suppose that we can, by exercising our reason eliminate any remaining undesired features by still more intelligent reflection, and still more appropriate design and 'rational coordination' of our undertakings. This leads one to be favorably disposed to central economic planning and control that lie at the heart of socialism."[53] Ignored by the "progressive" intellectual is the fact that there are other and more important elements that are at the root of and sustain our civilization. To these there seems to be a willful blindness. "How could," Hayek rhetorically asks, "traditions which people do not like and understand, whose effects they usually do not appreciate and can neither see nor foresee, and which they are still ardently combating, continue to have been passed on from generation to generation?" We owe to our religious heritage, Hayek concludes, that such beneficial traditions have been preserved and transmitted. From a purely naturalistic perspective, those traditions may be no more than "symbolic truths," but it has been and remains the role of religion in society to preserve our moral compass.

One must conclude that even at the end of his life, in spite of certain Aristotelian propensities, Hayek had not fully escaped the positivism of Auguste Comte and the Vienna Circle to which he had been exposed in his early years. Lacking a metaphysics, he remained confined to the phenomenal order of description and prediction. Still, like his mentor, Ludwig von Mises, it is to his lasting credit that he has alerted more than one generation to the main issue in social and political conflict, which is "whether a man should give away freedom, private initiative, and individual responsibility and surrender to the guardianship of a gigantic apparatus of compulsion and coercion, the socialist state."

Property as a Condition of Liberty

Attitudes with respect to the acquisition, use, and protection of property are but a manifestation of an unexpressed philosophy of human nature. It goes without saying that absent personal property be it real, intellectual, or monetary, one's scope of action is limited or nonexistent. But there is a deeper aspect to the holding of property that begs to be acknowledged. Ownership is closely tied to one's personal identity. A person is often known by his holdings, by the land that he owns, by the real estate or personal wealth that he has accumulated, and by the use he makes of it. Ownership is often an expression of taste and aspiration, of preferences tied to one's character. Property gives one a sense of independence and enables one to act in a multiplicity of ways otherwise impossible. Recreation, travel, the expansion of social contacts, the support of social and political activity, and the furtherance of one's education become possible. Absent appropriate financial resources, personal acumen is truncated.

If the advantages of property are so evident, how to account, in Western societies, for public acquiescence to the myriad government takings, from taxation to currency debasement, that effectively limit personal property and its use? The answer in part is that affirmations of the necessity of personal property usually carry with them an acknowledgment that from a moral point of view property carries with it certain obligations to the other. Given that an individual flourishes only within a community, it is universally recognized that a reciprocal relationship is created thereby, one that entails personal responsibility to the whole. This is the moral basis of taxation that goes beyond ordinary public services, for example, roads, utilities, and public parks, to alleviate the lot of the poor or the unfortunate. The concepts "social justice" and "social market economy" build on this moral mandate, as does public policy which seeks to implement objectives demanded in their name.

Discussions of the rights and duties of property owners date to antiquity. Property is so bound to considerations of human nature that the ancients still speak to us across the ages. Aristotle in his criticism of Plato's communal society recognized that private property, from an economic point of view, is more highly productive than communal ownership. Goods owned in common by a large number of people, Aristotle saw, will receive little attention since people will mainly pursue their own self-interest to the neglect of obligations they can pass off to others. Plato had argued in the *Republic* that communal ownership— or the leveling of property generally—would be conducive to peace since no one would then be envious of the other.[1] Aristotle responds to the contrary, noting that in general, living together and sharing in common all that matters is difficult, and most of all with regard to property[2] To impose communal property on society, he says, would be to disregard the record of human experience. In any communal effort, human nature being what it is, some people are likely work less than others and yet claim the same entitlement as those who work harder. Such, Aristotle held, can only lead to discontent and to fractional conflict. Aristotle also advances a moral consideration. Only private property enables one to practice the virtues of benevolence and philanthropy. Communal ownership would abolish that opportunity.

Plato and Aristotle apart, the most famous treatise on property from antiquity is that of Cicero, who begins with the observation that there is no such thing as private ownership established by nature. "Property becomes private either through long occupancy (as in the case of those who long ago settled in unoccupied territory) or through conquest (as in the case of those who took it in war), or by due process of law, bargain, or purchase, or by allotment. . . . Therefore, inasmuch as in each case some of those things which by nature had been common property became the property of individuals, each one should retain possession of that which has fallen to his lot; and if anyone appropriates to himself anything beyond that, he will be violating the laws of human society."[3] Property, however acquired, Cicero notes, is increased largely by wisdom, industry, and thrift and rightly belongs to its holder. Yet, says Cicero, as Plato reminds us, we are not born to ourselves alone. Our country and our friends make claims upon us. Fellowship requires that we help one another. "In this direction we ought to follow Nature as our guide, to contribute to the general good by an interchange of acts of kindness, by giving and receiving, and thus by our skill, our industry, and our talents to cement human society more closely together, man to man."[4]

Assistance to others must be rationally grounded, he continues. "For many people often do favors impulsively for everybody without discrimination, prompted by a morbid sort of benevolence or by a sudden impulse of the heart, shifting as the wind. Such acts of generosity are not to be so highly esteemed as those which are performed with judgment, deliberation, and mature consideration."[5]

"The man in an administrative office, however, must make it his first care that everyone shall have what belongs to him and that private citizens suffer no invasion of their property rights by act of the state."[6] "For . . . it is the peculiar function of the state and the city to guarantee to every man the free and undisturbed control of his own particular property."[7] Cicero speaks of destroyed harmony when property is taken away from one party and given to another or when officials intervene to cancel debt.

Although he speaks of the obligations of property holders, Cicero is clear that need does not create entitlement. Even so, he says, "let it [property] be made available for the use of as many as possible (if they are worthy) and be at the service of generosity and beneficence rather than sensuality and excess."[8] "Acquire, use, enjoy, and dispose, but rationally" is his time-transcending advice. Cicero's concept of "deserving poor" will be adopted by St. Jerome and St. Augustine and other Fathers of the Church when they speak of obligation in charity. They commonly affirm that charity to be efficacious cannot be mindless.

Ancient theories of property cannot effortlessly serve as a guide to the formation of law affecting property rights today, especially intellectual property, in our age of undreamt-of technological innovation. Even contemporary statutory law is hard pressed to resolve disputes over intellectual property rights.[9] Yet abstract discussions, ancient or contemporary, are not without consequence.

The idea that private property is at the root of political and economic evil is the well-known cornerstone of theories advanced by Marx and Engels. In *The Communist Manifesto*, Marx and Engels proclaim that the basis of communism as a theory may be summed up in a single sentence: abolition of private property.[10] The declared aim of Marx is the nationalization of economic assets for the common good. In a communist society, he tells us, everyone is to contribute according to his abilities and receive according to his needs. From this principle, the regulation of production is a *conditio sine qua non.*

John Stuart Mill, perhaps equally as influential as Marx, infused his brand of liberalism with the same socialist goal by stressing the overriding importance of the equitable distribution of productive wealth. Many of our contemporary intellectuals find in Mill the moral authority for legislation which curtails the right of ownership in the interest of the common good.[11]

Among the twentieth-century authors who treat property exclusively in moral terms, the most influential is undoubtedly John Rawls. In *A Theory of Justice* Rawls delineates what he believes to be the principles of a well-ordered society based on "fairness."[12] Rawls proposes to reform or abolish laws and institutions, no matter how efficient and well arranged, if they are "unjust." For Rawls, the essence of injustice is inequality. His ideal is perfect egalitarianism, a principle of equality that he applies not only to material goods but also to intelligence and inborn skills. The advantages afforded to the genetically favored ought not bring the fortunate possessor any special benefits. Why? Because they are unearned.[13] From Rawls's moral perspective, the allocation of talents and abilities must be regarded as "arbitrary." Talents should be viewed as "a common asset," and their possessors should profit from them "only on terms that improve the situation of those who have lost out." This principle was contested in an academic debate occasioned by the U.S. Supreme Court's consideration and subsequent ruling in *Eldred* v. *Ashcroft.*[14] The Court was asked to rule on the constitutionality of the Copyright Extension Act of 1998, which extended the limits of copyright beyond, it was contended, the constitutional specification of a limited time. The Court's ruling is a matter of record, and it is not our intent to review that ruling but to address the question: Does the larger society or community which may benefit from the productivity of an author or inventor have a just claim to the fruits of his labor? Rawls would say, yes.

Marx himself might have been shocked for Rawls goes far beyond even the most radical of communist theorists in wishing to socialize natural talents by denying to the talented the benefits their talents bring them. Rawls rejects "equality of opportunity" as inherently unfair since it means that the less gifted or less industrious will be left behind. Efficiency must be sacrificed in the name of equality.

It is to be noted that entitlements to what one has earned or otherwise legally acquired have a completely different status in *A Theory of Justice* than do freedom of speech, freedom of religion, freedom of association, due process of law, and the right to vote and to hold office. Property rights are excluded from protection. Economically significant property rights are valued not as conducive to liberty but as indispensable features of an economic system which must be maintained for the benefit of all. Reliance on contract, salary agreements, the payment of interest and dividends is economically essential, but its only moral justification is the good of the whole, not an individual's entitlement to what he has earned or otherwise acquired. What the individual is entitled to is determined by the overall system. Individual property rights are merely the consequence, not the foundation, of a just economic system.

Rawls, of course, is not the first in the history of political theory to take this extreme view. He acknowledges the influence of Rousseau and Hobbes, but his social view of property is more akin to that of that of Pierre Joseph Proudhon. In his famous treatise, *What is Property?*, Proudhon answers his own question with the memorable declaration, "Property is theft." Proudhon reasoned, as Rawls was to reason more than a century later, "All capital, whether material or mental, being the result of collective labor, is in consequence, collective property."[15]

But is it realistic to speak of the distribution of talents and the fruit of sometimes extraordinary individual or cooperative effort as a common asset? How far should distribution go? In *The Law of Peoples*, Rawls proposes the extension of his principles of justice to the Society of Peoples under the Law of Peoples. "The Law of Peoples," he writes, "is an extension of the liberal conception of justice for a domestic regime to a Society of Peoples."[16] It is not the intent of this brief presentation to offer a detailed critique of Rawls but to suggest that a seemingly benevolent theory of justice, viewed in terms of its consequence, can lead us to utopian ideals far removed from reality. In advancing his theory of justice, Rawls ignores psychological, political, and economic realities as well as recorded history and the findings of anthropologists.

Without explicitly addressing Rawls, the French political theorist, Pierre Manent, meets Rawls's concept of a global "Society of Peoples" head-on. In *Democracy Without Nations: The Fate of Self-Government in Europe*, Manent argues that the democratic nation is the irreplaceable political context for human action, the instrument of self-government, the locus for deliberation, and the administration of justice.[17] He shows that after Maastricht the European Union's bureaucratic contrivances have become more and more artificial, detached from the national political bodies that formed the Union, and have taken on a life of their own. Instead of increasing self-governance, Europe's new instruments of governance shackle it ever more with each passing day, promising an indefinite extension that no one wills and no one knows how to stop. In Manent's judgment, Europe's governing classes, without explicitly saying so, hope to create a homogeneous and limitless human world. In fact, he continues, given its intellectual climate, what distinguishes Europeans from one another cannot be evaluated or even publically named. The European value that seems to trump all others is "openness to the other," a universal political creed that relegates to the private sphere religious belief and cultural identity. "We [Europeans] do not possess any particular existence," Manent writes. "We do not want to possess any shape, manner or form, a distinctive character of our own, one that would necessarily be particular."[18] To parry the threat of self-destruction, Manent is convinced that nothing is more important than to get a grip on our centuries-old development and that means first of all that we must become fully aware of the original Christian character of our nations.

Clearly ideas advanced within the academic sector are not without consequence in the social and political order. The effect of ideologically induced welfare programs adopted in the West in the 1930s and in the post-World War II period is now being felt on both sides of the Atlantic. All such programs required immense monetary outlays that could only be attained through taxation of one form or another. The cultural historian, Richard Pipes, in his authoritative study, *Property and Freedom,* dramatically shows how modern democratic governments have become giant mechanisms for the redistribution of private assets to the disadvantage of personal freedom.[19] He shows that the United States, for example, in its desire to alleviate the lot of the poor has gone beyond that goal in its quest to "abolish poverty itself." In the pursuit of the latter objective, policy has moved from a guarantee of equality of opportunity to equality of results. Pipes dates this transformation to President Lyndon Johnson, whom he regards as the principal architect of the postwar welfare state in the United States. In an address at Howard University, June 1965, Johnson asserted, "Freedom is not enough. . . we seek not just freedom but opportunity. . . not just equality as a right and a theory but as a fact and as a result."[20] Pipes comments, "It is doubtful that either Johnson and his speech writers or the public at large had any inkling of what a break with the Western tradition these words represented. Social equality can be attained, if at all, only by coercion, that is at the expense of liberty. It necessarily requires the violation of property rights of those citizens who posses more wealth or enjoy higher societal status than the majority. Once the elimination of poverty becomes a state objective, the state is bound to treat property not as a fundamental right, which is its supreme obligation to protect, but as an obstacle to social justice."[21] Pipes goes on to point out that "Liberty is by its nature inegalitarian, because living creatures differ in strength, intelligence, ambition, courage, perseverance and all else that makes for success."[22]

Economic historians tell us that those countries that have provided the firmest guarantees of economic independence, especially property rights, are virtually without exception the richest. For most economic historians the determinant of economic growth lies in the legal institutions which ensure to enterprising individuals the fruits of their labors. European history suggests that the rise of the West to the position of global economic preeminence lies in the institution of private property.[23]

Romantic appeals to the common good, such as those of Mill and Rawls, may be fruitful under some conditions, but absent a sense of community, they are dangerous. As Richard Pipes reminds us, when one appeals to a common good separate from and superior to the private goods of individuals, the function of government (be it that of a legislative, executive, or judiciary body) becomes one of conflict management. Given our litigious society, opposing parties are likely to press for state-awarded privileges, bargaining and negotiating for advantage. Under such conditions the state is not likely to represent a common will, but rather it becomes the object of adversarial wills. Thus positioned, the state serves not by defining goals which members of society ought collectively to pursue but by removing obstacles to goods privately defined. The common good becomes the result of negotiations between private political actors. Such a situation can only lead to social and economic disaster. A compliant or weak judiciary is apt to rule in the light of a supposed common good against an individual claimant, perhaps settling the dispute but undermining other fundamental rights.

The issue before us remains: What claim does society have on the individual? Ancient notions of human nature are the foundation of the common-law tradition assumed in the English-speaking world, a tradition that informed the documents associated with the American founding. The U.S. Constitution took for granted that the right to private property is a condition of liberty. It was taken as evident that property rights adhere not only to the individual but also to the individual in his collective arrangements. If a man is entitled to the fruit of his labor, a corporation is entitled to the fruit of its investment. Apart from the judgment rendered by the Supreme Court in *Eldred* v. *Ashcroft*,[24] cited above, one is brought to the conclusion that Article 1, Section 8 of the U.S. Constitution had it right when it declared its purpose ". . . to promote the progress of science and the useful arts, by securing for limited times to authors and inventors the exclusive rights to their respective writings and discoveries." The Constitution provides a prudential balance between the protection of property rights and social claims. There may always be a tension between property rights and reasonable communal claims. There may always be a tension between property rights and reasonable communal claims. Resolution in the practical order cannot avoid an appeal to an undergirding philosophy of human nature. Ultimately the conflict may be between the common-sense philosophy of Aristotle and the Stoics and that of Karl Marx and others of the Enlightenment period.

Tolerance: Virtue or Vice

I

When Oswald Spengler published his multivolume study, *The Decline of the West*, few outside of professional academic circles understood his thesis or took the epitaph seriously.[1] Today, three-quarters of a century later, no attentive historian can ignore the cultural shift that has taken place within the West in the last half of the twentieth century. As a philosopher of history, Spengler's study of the past and his cyclical view of history led him to the pessimistic conclusion that just as other cultures before it have decayed, Western culture has not only peaked but faces a period of irreversible decline.

For more than two hundred years the Western intellectual tradition has been subjected to the nihilistic criticism of forces launched by the Enlightenment. The result: the West is now experiencing in the social order the fruit of the eighteenth-century repudiation of the classical and Christian sources of Western culture. There is little doubt that Europe is living off a dying past, perhaps nearing the end of a great culture, not unlike that experienced before the fall of Rome when internal corruption made possible the barbarian invasion. The decline of morals apart, the birthrate of the native European population alone would attest to decline.

In spite of evidence to the contrary, the ruling elites of Brussels and the European capitals seem confident that the constitutive elements of what was once called "Christendom" can be maintained without reference to their source. Addressing what he sees as a gap between Brussels and the national identity of the peoples who make up the European union, the French political theorist Pierre Manent writes, "Europe's political contrivances have become more and more artificial. With each day they recede further from the natural desires and movements of their citizens' souls." Enlightened despotism, he fears, has returned in the form of agencies, administrations, courts of justice, and commissions that lay down the law, or create rules ever more meticulously contrived. Sovereignty is not only challenged by Brussels but threatened by the power of judges to elevate "rights claims" at the expense of political authority.[2]

Absent Christianity, Europe has little to defend but its material culture as it faces a tide of immigrants that threaten its very character. The newcomers, largely from Africa and the Middle East, who are attracted by the material culture of Europe, nevertheless remain attached to their old ways and in refusing to assimilate extract privileges and exceptions to the common law that further contributes to their isolation within the larger society, The question arises, how tolerant can Europe be in the face of a largely Muslim influx whose Islamic leaders are convinced that they will one day rule the continent.

Are we driven to Spengler's pessimistic conclusion, albeit for different reasons? Perhaps not. In any event, intellectual honesty demands that we acknowledge the many formidable obstacles confronting not only the defense of Europe but of Western culture itself as it faces an alien and self-confident Islam convinced that it will one day govern. Those bold enough to predict the future foresee an "Islamic Republic of France" or the inevitability of what Bat Ye'Or has called "Eurabia," but those authors are given little credence, are largely ignored by major media, and can expect their books to be banned or removed from the shelves of major booksellers. Absent the classical moral and intellectual resources which prevailed, for example, in the decades preceding the founding of the American republic, Europe's ruling elites may be hard-pressed to defend the republican institutions and the culture they have taken for granted. On both sides of the Atlantic, any effort to recapture the moral tradition that shaped the colonial Declaration of Independence and the U.S. Constitution as well as the U.N. Universal Declaration of Human Rights is handicapped by the current propensity to regard all moral claims as equal. The concept of "procedural democracy," now regnant in the United States, militates against the government's casting its weight behind any one conception of the good. The state according to this mode of thinking must remain neutral in the face of competing moral claims, favoring none. No moral system can claim superiority, it is argued, since each is merely the product of its time and of the place-bound preferences of people advancing it.

Procedural democracy itself is supported by two ancillary principles, one, the seemingly innocent call for "tolerance," and the other, the malevolent doctrine of "separation of church and state," which reduces religion to a private devotion. The principle of tolerance augurs against an unabashed defense of one's own tradition, whereas the separation principle surrenders moral authority to the state or, worse still, is employed to eradicate religion from both the academy and the public square. To offer an egregious example of misplaced tolerance, one may recall that the 57-member Muslim Organization of the Islamic Conference (OIC) has prevailed upon the United Nations Human Rights Commission to adopt a resolution requiring the effective evisceration of the Universal Declaration of Human Rights. Henceforth, the guaranteed right of free expression will not extend to any criticism of Islam on the grounds that it amounts to an abusive act of religious discrimination. A Pakistan agency has in 2010 instituted a "media watch," whose purpose is to identify media outlets that promulgate material deemed offensive to Islam. Western officials and governmental agencies appear increasingly disposed to go along with efforts to mute warnings about the danger that the recognition or incorporation of Sharia law poses to the West. The liberal attempt to silence criticism of Islam threatens to criminalize behavior that has long been regarded as merely "politically incorrect."[3]

II

Calls for tolerance abound, from papal statements to European conferences. Bumper stickers and postal imprints proclaim its value. One can understand John Paul II and Benedict XVI seeking tolerance for a Christian minority living amongst a largely Hindu population, but one is mystified by an apparent campaign for tolerance in the open societies of Western Europe, Australia, and North America. Considered abstractly, it would be easier to make the case that tolerance is a vice than to justify its putative status as a virtue. To employ a few homey examples: a parent cannot tolerate disobedience in the child; a teacher, sloppy homework or cheating on an examination; a military officer, insubordination;

a CEO, deviance from company policy; or an ecclesiastical body, divergent doctrinal teaching or liturgical practice within its ranks. No state can tolerate irresponsible fiscal policy nor can any state permit disrespect for its laws. An entity must preserve its unity to preserve its very being.

The promotion of the notion that tolerance is a virtue is of enlightenment origin. Some trace its origin to Descartes, others to Spinoza, and still others to Luther and Calvin.[4] Tolerance is not mentioned as a virtue by Aristotle or by the Stoics. Nor does Aquinas speak of tolerance as a virtue. To the contrary, Roget's venerable *English Language Dictionary of Synonyms and Antonyms* gives as synonyms for tolerance: leniency, clemency, indulgence, laxity, sufferance, concession, and permissiveness, terms generally regarded as designating questionable behavior.

Of course, certain technical meanings of the term may be identified. "Tolerance" in biology is the ability of an organism to endure contact with a substance or its introduction into the body without ill effects. "Tolerance" in the industrial order is the range within which a dimension of a machined part may vary. "Religious tolerance," which many have in mind when they use the term, is the intellectual and practical acknowledgment of the right of others to live in accordance with religious beliefs different from one's own.

Religious tolerance, though not confined to Christianity, seems to have a particular appeal to the Christian conscience. Perhaps it does so for reasons intrinsic to Christianity itself. Hindus and Muslims, by contrast, show no similar tolerance toward Christians in their midst, either subjugating them or forcing them to flee. The classical and biblical sources of Western civilization may still remain the basis of Western culture, but that said, it must be acknowledged that the Western respect for intellect and for its role in the formation of law and the practice of religion is not characteristic of all who seek shelter within the West. Social cohesion becomes impossible if the classical and biblical heritage of the West is not respected by the immigrant whose enfranchisement can be used to undermine the institutions and freedoms of the host country. The call for a tolerance that ignores a de facto conflict of cultures is inconsistent and destructive of its own warrant. We may ask, is it not incumbent upon the West to defend its intellectual and cultural patrimony while yet accommodating the other?

Goethe, when discussing tolerance in his *Maxims and Reflections*,[5] offers this insightful distinction. Tolerance, he thinks, is best understood as a state of mind in transition to something nobler, namely, "recognition." The latter is a mark of true liberality, an attitude equally removed from mindless appropriation and the outright rejection of the other's point of view or culture. The recognition of those who think and act differently is a feature of a confident mind. Upon our first encounter with another, we may derive pleasure in finding points of agreement, in a feeling of good will that follows a friendly contact. Upon closer acquaintance, differences are likely to become apparent. The important thing, says Goethe, is not to retreat but to hold fast to points of agreement and strive for a clear understanding of points of dispute without seeking an artificial agreement on them.

Throughout history, political entities have recognized the need for unity of outlook among their peoples. At times in classical Greece and Rome, atheism could be punished by death. Modern socialist regimes, whenever they come to power, recognize the influence of ideas and work to suppress religious education, if not religion itself. Within the Western democracies practical accommodation is one thing, but a non-judgmental, nondiscriminating acceptance is another. How tolerant can a society be and yet maintain itself in existence? Of course, where nothing is prized, everything can be tolerated.

III

"Procedural democracy," as currently defended in academic circles, rests upon the assumption that there is no way to determine the good. The state in formulating its policies is not to draw upon any one moral tradition, certainly not on one advanced from a purely religious perspective or by an ecclesial body. Religion is deemed a purely private or subjective affair, not a trustworthy source of principles applicable to public policy. In this context, particularly in the United States, the separation doctrine is often invoked, but that doctrine is not found in the U.S. Constitution. It is rather the construct of a maverick interpretation of the U.S. Supreme Court acquiescing to the secular humanists who vigorously lobbied the Court. Any student of the American founding will recognize that the Constitution in its First Amendment sought only to prevent an established church for the nation as a whole and did not intend to undo establishment in the colonies where it prevailed. It doesn't take much research to discover that at the outbreak of the American Revolution there were established churches in nine of the thirteen colonies. At the time of the founding the positive role of religion in society was simply taken for granted. It was commonly recognized that man is by nature a spiritual and a material being and that government should not impede growth in either domain.

As a principle, religious tolerance prevails throughout the West, but the battle to shape the common mind has been shifted from the pulpit to the classroom. While John Locke, David Hume, and Adam Smith favored religious establishment, their contemporary disciples, recognizing the need for civic unity, are in the forefront of those who would achieve that unity by giving the state exclusive control over education. Whereas David Hume maintained that, "The union of civil and ecclesiastical power serves extremely, in even civilized government, to the maintenance of peace and order," and Blackstone could hold that uniformity in religious matters is a civic good, contemporary defenders of "establishment" have shifted their focus to the control of education, effectively denying parents a choice in the education of their children. In the United States, in the name of separating church and state, the choice of a religiously informed education, though not denied outright, is rendered financially difficult if not impossible for most families at the crucial primary and secondary levels.

Unfortunately with the dismissal of religion often goes that other support of republican government, the classical learning which informed the political philosophy of the founding fathers of the American republic. At the time of the American founding, Cicero's discourses framed the issues that were addressed in the Declaration of Independence and the U.S. Constitution, topics such as liberty, the nature and source of law, the common good, security, patriotism, toleration, and the role of religion in society. Eighteenth-century readers understood Cicero to be a defender of rectitude, virtue and conservative customs and the indispensable role which religion plays in fostering these values. For Cicero, the highest aim of the ruler is the security and welfare of the community because the common welfare is the indispensable condition for personal advancement. Security justifies the use of force against aggressors, but the maintenance of morality in the populace is also a fundamental responsibility of the ruler. The ruler, of necessity, must be able to distinguish between what is truly good (the *bonum honestum*) and what is merely expedient (the *bonum utile*). Cicero acknowledges that from one point of view, the pursuit of the *bonum honestum* is but a means for the realization of the common good in which it finds its purpose and limit; this makes *honestum* a form of *utile*. But Cicero also identifies *honestum* with the common good and *utile* with individual interest. To what extent, then, is the common good to be pursued against the interest of the individual?

This is the issue which confronts policy makers throughout the West. No ancient text can provide a ready answer to contemporary problems, yet the ancients can speak to us across the ages about human fulfillment and the ends of government. In his own day when he wrote of a failing Rome, Livy recommended to his contemporaries the study of its founding.

> I invite the reader's attention to the much more serious consideration of the kind of lives our ancestors lived, of who were the men and what the means, both in politics and war, by which Rome's power was first acquired and subsequently expanded. I would have him trace the processes of our moral decline, to watch first the sinking of the foundations of morality as the old teaching was allowed to lapse, then the final collapse of the whole edifice, and the dark dawning of our modern day when we can neither endure our vices nor face the remedies needed to cure them.[6]

Respect for ancestry, heritage, or tradition determines concretely the emphasis placed on the study of history, languages, art, and on the observance of religious and civic ritual. Failure to appreciate and defend the uniqueness of the moral and spiritual traditions of what was once called "Christendom" or in the name of tolerance treat them as only one among many can only end, as Spengler predicted, in the suicide of the West.

Benedict XVI could have been taking a page from Livy when he touched on these issues in his 2008 visit to Paris and again in his October visit to the Quirinal Palace in Rome. Assembled to hear him at the Bernardines, the ancient Cistercian abbey in Paris, were the leading civic leaders of the French republic, including the minister of culture, two former presidents, Valéry Giscard d'Estaing and Jacques Chirac, and the current mayor of Paris. Given the setting of his lecture, Benedict said, "We are in a place that is associated with the culture of monasticism," reminding his listeners of the Benedictine "l'amour des lettres et le desir de Dieu," and the role that monasticism played in the development of Western civilization. He went on to speak of the nature of the Church herself and of European culture. "A purely positive culture," he said, "which drives the question of God into the subjective realm, as being unscientific, would be the renunciation of reason, the renunciation of its highest possibilities, and hence a disaster for humanity with very grave consequences. That gave Europe's culture its foundations—the search for God and the readiness to listen to Him—remains today the basis for any genuine culture."

Prime Minister François Fillon, in his farewell remarks to the Holy Father, told Benedict that he had reminded them that "the fundamental separation of church and state does not prevent either from dialoging or from being mutually enriched." The prime minister spoke of an "open and reflective secularism" and stated, "The republic, profoundly secular, respects the existence of the religious fact. She appreciates the role of the Christian tradition in her history and her cultural and immaterial heritage." He thanked Benedict for "placing our civilization on guard regarding its material weakness." A weak acknowledgment of the role of religion in society, to be sure, but nevertheless an expression of what President Sarkozy has called a "more positive laicité." As a militant Islamic presence in Europe increases, even Brussels' secular elites may be faced with the limits of tolerance and the handicap imposed by their commitment to procedural democracy.

Responsibility: Recognition and Limits

Acknowledging that global economic integration is moving at an unprecedented pace, the chairman of the U.S. Federal Reserve System, Ben S. Bernanke, in a 2006 address urged policy makers to ensure that the benefits of globalization are widely shared. Although his statement was almost a literal quotation from John Paul II, Bernanke's motive was purely financial, a desire to stem protectionist sentiment in the disadvantaged trading partner.[1] One cannot fault his reasoning, exploitation may not pay in the long run. When F. A. Hayek addressed the phenomenon of globalization almost seventy-five years ago, he feared the power and exploitation that usually flowed from foreign investment.

Economic and other data show clearly the gap between the "developed world" and the so-called "developing world," between rich nations and poor nations. The poverty and misery characteristic of the latter are shown daily on worldwide television. The data recognized, the moral judgment is made; those that have, should do something to alleviate the lot of the have-nots. Churchmen talk about a fair distribution of the earth's goods without reference to how those goods are produced, let alone how they might be distributed. Responsibility of the first world to the third world is taken for granted. "Rich nations," "first world," "developed world" are abstractions, yet they support the notion that somehow one collective is responsible for or to another collective.

On the occasion of the 2006 meeting of the G-7, the Center for Global Development released data to show that the commitment of rich countries to the world's poorest nations is slipping. The center maintains a "Commitment to Development Index" and ranks nations according to a set of criteria that reflects national policies and the amount of aid proffered in proportion to the size of the donor's economy. In the judgment of Dennis Roodman, designer of the Index, all nations including the highest could do better. The United States judged in absolute terms with respect to the amount of aid rendered ranks last on the environmental component of the Index because of low gasoline

taxes that purportedly encourage consumption and because of per-capi-
ta greenhouse gas emissions that are second only to Australia's among
rich nations. Speaking of the G-7, Roodman says "From what was
needed to what was promised, the results are disappointing."[2] Whatever
one thinks of Roodman's index, the underlying assumption is that the
rich nations have a responsibility vis-á-vis the poor nations of the world
and should feel guilty for not doing more.

Readiness to accept the notion of "collective responsibility" and its
correlative "collective guilt," no doubt, stems from discussions following a number of egregious cases where societies taken as a whole seem
accountable. The twentieth century provides numerous examples of
societies' acting, if not as a whole, at least with sufficient unity, to
implement morally unacceptable policy, i.e., Germany under Hitler, the
Soviet Union under Stalin, both governments systematically eliminat-
ing so-called "enemies of the state." One thinks also of South Africa's
limiting full civic participation to whites, of the antebellum American
South enslaving the blacks, and the post-bellum American South
enacting segregation laws. To what extent are we willing to blame the
German or Soviet peoples for the atrocities committed within the
borders of their nations? Can the nineteenth-century immigrant cooper
working within his shop in Minneapolis be blamed for slavery or for
post-bellum statutes enacted with the South? The way we talk about
these matters may contribute to misunderstanding. We speak of "sharing in the greatness of a nation," we may say that "we take pride in
belonging to a scholarly family," but we must be careful not to hyposta-
tize abstractions or make them bearers of a value. Linguistic devices
that make for succinctness of expression are to be recognized for their
metaphorical and elliptical meaning and not taken for literal truth.[3] A
family group or nation, I am willing to argue, cannot be the bearer of
guilt: in neither is there sufficient unity or participation in the deliber-
ative process to warrant accountability.

Corporations are different. They are not mere aggregates of people
but have a metaphysical-logical identity. Otto von Gierke has suggested that the law in conferring on the corporation the status of a legal
person is merely recognizing a prelegal, social condition. The corporation is the result of certain social actions and possesses a de facto

personality that the law declares to be a juridical fact.[4] Brian Tierney traces the notion of corporate personality to medieval canon law and its doctrine of agency. "In Roman law," writes Tierney, "an individual or group could appoint an agent to negotiate with a third party, but the result of the transaction was to establish an obligation between the third party and the agent, not directly between the third party and the principal. In canon law, when a corporate group established a representative with *plena potestas,* the group was directly obligated by the representative's acts even when it had not consented to them in advance."[5] The ancient Roman principle, *Quod omnes tangit ab omnibus approbatur* (what touches all is to be approved by all), was to be replaced by one that allowed a representative to act on behalf of all. Thus commitments made in the name of an organized group may persist even after the composition of the group or its will changes. If a group reneges on a commitment, the fault may be that of no individual member, yet the liability for the breach of contract, falling on the group as a whole, will distribute burdens quite unavoidably on faultless members.

Peter A. French, in an extended analysis of corporate responsibility, maintains that for a corporation to be treated as a moral person, it must be possible to attribute to it a corporate intention. This is different from attributing intentions to biological persons who comprise its board of directors or its top level management.[6] Corporations, at least major corporations, have internal decision-making structures, and this arrangement is reflected in their organizational charts and in their established methods of reaching corporate policy. French believes that in many cases one can infer the basic beliefs of a corporation by examining its actions over a period of time. The moment policy is sidestepped or violated, it is no longer the policy of the company. Maverick acts cannot be described as having been done for corporate reasons. Thus it is possible to distinguish between individual staff negligence and corporate negligence. Executives voting to adopt certain objectives when required by the corporate structure to vote, in fact, constitutes the corporation's deciding to do something. A corporate officer who ignores corporate policy, possibly in the name of expediency, may be morally accountable without moral blame's being attached to the corporation, although corporate civil accountability may be unavoidable.

These principles apply to the military occupation of Iraq and to famous cases such as the *Exxon Valdez* oil spill and more recent oil spills off the coast of France and Spain. In the aftermath of the *Exxon Valdez* oil spill, the U.S. National Wildlife Federation urged prosecutors to go after the individual at the top of the corporation who was responsible for the accident. In due course the former skipper of the Valdez and its owner Exxon itself were criminally charged.

It is not surprising to find that following the close of World War II there were numerous discussions of collective responsibility and guilt as the Allied officials debated humanitarian policy vis-a-vis a fallen foe. The literature, of course, is enormous, but a few examples will illustrate the dominant American position at that time that has some bearing on the present discussion. Judge Robert H. Jackson, the American member of the team prosecuting the Nazis at Nuremberg, in his address at the opening of the trial, repudiated the notion of collective responsibility.[7] "Jackson made it clear," writes Suzanne Brown-Fleming, that "it would be unjust to indict all German people, women and children who had no voice in domestic politics, as well as to indict the countless number of anti-Nazis, many of whom suffered years in concentration camps."[8] General Robert A. McClure took a similar approach. The U.S. Army, he thought, should approach the German people not on the basis of guilt and punishment, but rather on the basis of cause and consequence.[9] General Dwight Eisenhower condemned a policy of vengeance and called for a fair dealing with a fallen foe.[10] Bernard Baruch, an advisor to Franklin D. Roosevelt, had taken the opposite view. Many thought that a distinction had to be made between guilt and responsibility, one that would permit a claim for reparations without the necessity of establishing guilt on the part of the German populace as a whole. I will return momentarily to the distinction between responsibility and guilt.

Other examples imputing collective guilt may be offered. When the New World was celebrating the 500th anniversary of Columbus's 1492 voyage, dissident voices emerged to condemn the colonization that followed. It was not uncommon to find not only Christopher Columbus but European civilization as a whole condemned for all the ills that befell the native population in the years following the discovery of

America. The "affirmative action" movement in the United States may be taken as an example of one generation's assuming responsibility for the sins of another. Peoples, generations, classes, races, industries and religious bodies are often held accountable, not in some vague "public opinion sort of way," but before courts of law. From tort law as practiced in the United States to affirmative action policy, blame is often assigned to groups no longer in existence and sometimes to mere conceptual entities. Restitution is not infrequently extracted from groups or from heirs of groups without any responsibility for harms being established.

To cite one notorious example from the United States that may have its counterpart in Europe: Consider the concept "market share" where corporate defendants may be assessed damage even after proving that they could not possibly have caused the harm. Courts in several states have employed market share in cases where several corporations that are marketing essentially the same product are held responsible for harm done to a plaintiff who does not remember whose product was used. Damages are in such cases distributed among the manufacturers on the basis of their percentage of the market, with no concrete responsibility having been established. Broad notions entertained in the framing and implementation of law are almost always the byproduct of previous academic discussion. Before the concept of market share could have become current, certain philosophical discussions of collective guilt, collective responsibility, and punishment had to take place. While this is not the place to examine the history of all of these concepts, little inquiry is needed to show that the notion of collective guilt is an ancient one. In fact, discussions of that notion can be found in ancient and medieval texts as well as modern and contemporary literature.

The ancients no less than we recognized that societies are generated out of collective beliefs and traditions that are passed unconsciously by individuals. Emile Durkheim, the influential social theorist of the late 19th century, was convinced that traditions can exist in groups even when they are not instantiated by any individual. In his *Rules of Sociological Method* (1895) he even accords ontological status to social traditions and social relations independent of individual members of

the group.[11] In an influential volume written shortly after the close of
World War II, Karl Jaspers attempted to deal with guilt of the German
nation.[12] The horrors perpetrated in the concentration camps were by
then generally known. What was suspected had become graphically
illustrated. Jaspers raised the question of guilt in the context of
demands for restitution. To what extent were the German people as a
whole culpable, and to what extent could one expect atonement? The
issue was not that of the responsibility of the German state. No one
questioned national accountability or the requirement of "reparations."
Jaspers was probing much deeper. In a section entitled "Scheme of
Distinctions," Jaspers, like the Allied Command, was aware that the
vast majority of German-speaking peoples were not morally responsible for the atrocities committed under the Third Reich. If the vast
majority of the German people were neither legally nor morally guilty,
could the German-speaking peoples yet be held accountable? In an
effort to sort things out, Jaspers introduced the notion of "collective
guilt at the psychic level." He reasoned that insofar as the German people shared a common language and a common culture and insofar as
they were nourished by a common literature, common music and
distinctive patterns of civic behavior, they could be said to be a collective. In Jaspers's analysis there existed enough solidarity to produce a
national psyche that in some sense could be held accountable such that
one generation could make claims on another. Jaspers recognized the
difficulty of defending a notion of psychological guilt apart from criminal, political, or moral guilt. He preferred to call it "metaphysical
guilt." Having distinguished the four concepts of guilt,[13] Jaspers, in the
concluding pages of his book, writes, "A crime is atoned for; a political liability is limited by a peace treaty and thus brought to an end. . . .
But moral and metaphysical guilt, understood only by the individual in
his community, are by their very nature not atoned for. They do not
cease. Whoever bears them enters into a process lasting all his life."[14]
"There exists," he believed, "a solidarity among men as human beings
that makes each co-responsible for every wrong and every injustice in
the world, especially for crimes committed in his presence or with his
knowledge. If I fail to do whatever I can to prevent them, I too am
guilty. If I was present at the murder of others without risking my life

to prevent it, I feel guilty in a way not adequately conceivable either legally, politically or morally."[15] Elsewhere, in a puzzling remark that undermines his theses, he concedes, "There is no such thing as a people as a whole."[16]

Jaspers was only one among many theologians who in the aftermath of the war began rethinking the notions of "responsibility," "guilt," and "restitution." On the American side of the Atlantic, Aloisius Muench, Bishop of Fargo, South Dakota, devoted his Lenten Pastoral Letter in 1946 to the European situation.[17] In his pastoral letter entitled "One World in Charity" Muench objected to official policy, "official inhumanity," he called it, "which does not permit the United Nations Relief and Rehabilitation Administration to ship relief supplies to either Germany or Japan, and besides does not even allow private relief agencies to send and distribute food, clothing, and medicine to war-stricken people living a pitiable life in the ruins of their bombed-out cities."[18] In Europe, policy dictated that refugees from the East were to be taken care of first. The needs of the German people were to be considered last, and only then was aid to be given to avoid disease or the possibility of insurrection.[19] Muench was equally critical of Nazism and Communism, as well as the Allied bombing responsible for the holocaust inflicted on the German populace.

Reflecting on the issues raised by the foregoing, we have laid bare a number of distinctions and assumptions. No one denies that guilt implies responsibility. Responsibility in turn presupposes freedom to act or not to act. In speaking of freedom, it is necessary to distinguish (1) between freedom in a moral sense and freedom under the law, and (2) between the legal sense of guilt and the moral sense. One can be accountable before civil law without being morally responsible for harm. Civil law itself recognizes this when it takes into consideration motivation and extenuating circumstances and sometimes allows them to mitigate guilt. The continuity between the moral and the civil is so connected that in practice the distinction is often blurred or ignored. Moral outrage is not infrequently thought to be immediately translatable into law. Appeals for the creation of law typically invoke danger to health or damage to the environment or cite other material or social disadvantage if action is not taken, but they are, nonetheless, appeals to the moral order.

Another aspect to keep in mind is that action follows judgment and that judgment is made necessarily within a cultural context. How one views a proposed course of action is in part dependent on one's education, i.e., the distinctions one has learned to make and the principles one invokes habitually. Certain courses of action may be acceptable in the West that are unthinkable in the East. In the West some may see nothing wrong with the merchandising of pornography, with divorce, or with abortion. The same is not true in a strict Islamic society. It would be precarious to attribute moral guilt to those who act in the light of conscience, even if that conscience, when judged by a time-transcending moral code, seems to be ill-informed. But this does not mean that holders are unaccountable for their beliefs in all respects. From any point of view one has an obligation to form a correct conscience.

Also recognized is the principle that not all law binds in conscience. Good civil law, as we have suggested, tends to explicate or elaborate the moral order. Thus building codes, traffic regulations, and rules governing securities trading are in some sense moral dictates before they become statutes. Law that flouts common perceptions of right and wrong is not regarded as morally binding. The distinction between civil law and moral law, although sometimes challenged from the academy, is universally recognized. The distinction cuts both ways. A corporation that operates wholly within the law may be guilty of moral infraction. The sale of pornography, the creation of advertising that deliberately manipulates the truth, or media distortion on behalf of partisan causes are examples to the point. One can make the claim that the manufacturing of faux merchandise, merchandise that mimics the genuine article and is usually marketed to the ill-educated or unsuspecting, is a kind of moral infraction. Some would extend guilt to those who manufacture tobacco products or distilled spirits or make clothing from animal pelts. No one would hesitate to attribute moral guilt to a corporation that knowingly manufactures a defective and potentially dangerous product, quite apart from any civic penalty that might be inflicted.

To come to the point: granted immorality on the part of a corporation, where does moral guilt lie? Are all who are associated with the corporation collectively guilty? If not, how far down the corporate ladder does responsibility extend? To the worker on the assembly line? To the wholesaler? To the retailer? To the shareholder? If guilt follows knowledge, it may be that only a few in the testing laboratory or in the executive suite are privy to the information that a given product is potentially troublesome or could be modified with additional cost to diminish risk. Although the corporation before the law can be held accountable for negligence, it is difficult to believe that the average worker in the plant or billing office, unless the company has a record of dubious performance, has the knowledge that would imply criminal complicity. There are exceptions of course. Complicity may be much more widespread or deeper than is sometimes thought. We have all read stories of whistle blowers who, rather than be complicit, have brought to light questionable practices, sometimes to the gratitude of management. Where corporate guilt is determined, it is not likely that all workers would be held accountable either by an irate group of shareholders or before a court of law. When a specific individual, in violation of corporate policy, has been guilty of harm, it makes little sense to hold the corporation criminally liable, subject to punitive damages that are ultimately shared by innocent shareholders.

Jaspers, in his treatise on German guilt, would likely recognize all of these principles, yet he held that the German-speaking populace could not avoid what he called "metaphysical guilt." The currency of this notion does not date to antiquity, and it is certainly not found in the tradition of Aristotle and Aquinas. Psychological or metaphysical guilt in Jaspers's sense is something self-inflicted, subjectively generated, known only to God and to the sinner. It is not accountable to some universally recognized moral order. Theologians may speak of the "stain of sin," but the Calvinist and the Catholic may have different things in mind when talking about punishment due to sin. If there are no outside standards by which the conscience can be measured, metaphysical guilt becomes an indelible ontological disposition that not even therapy can remove. The Catholic may confess, repent, do penance and leave it all behind. Subjectively imposed guilt is indelible and can be exploited by others to gain concessions both of an ideological and material sort.

Returning to the notion of responsibility apart from the guilt question, in what sense are "those who have" responsible for "those who have not?" Indeed, what are the obligations or responsibility of rich nations to poor nations? As I write, one encounters daily appeals for the poor of Somalia and Darfur. The Christian may recognize an obligation in charity that the agnostic may not. Cardinal Muench, in condemning allied policy in the aftermath of World War II, could explicitly invoke Christian principles of compassion, mercy, and charity to positive effect. The vengeful Morgenthau Plan was rejected by President Truman, and Morgenthau's resignation was immediately accepted when precipitously offered on the eve of the Potsdam Conference.[20] Social philosophers, such as Emile Durkheim and John Dewey, have long recognized the motivating power of religion in confronting the difficult good. In a largely secular milieu, are appeals to charity possible? Dorothy Sayers would answer, "yes." In her 1947 Oxford lecture, "The Lost Tools of Learning," she noticed "that many people today who are atheist or agnostic in religion are governed in their conduct by a code of Christian ethics which is so rooted (in the culture) that it never occurs to them to question it." She then adds, aware of the Enlightenment's influence on Western intellectuals, "But one cannot live on capital forever."[21]

When "obligation in charity" cannot be invoked, we find pragmatic appeals on the basis of self-interest; that and emotional appeals accompanied by graphic depictions of need that beg for remedy. Acknowledging that both pragmatic and emotional appeals often fail, the United Nations has sought the power to tax to alleviate recognized need. Whereas charity is rational, imposing its own limits, emotional appeals tend to be unrestrained and often impulsively lead to inappropriate action and squandered resources.

The gap between the "developed world" and the "developing world" is not likely to be bridged anytime soon. Chairman Bernanke's call to avoid exploitation is nothing other than a call for justice, a call for responsible behavior, but apart from treating them justly, the question remains: does that make rich nations responsible for poor ones? In spite of the social determinism favored by the political left, we still recognize the principle of self-reliance, a principle that analogically may be applied to nations.

If we have reached any conclusion, it is this: responsibility cannot be assigned willy-nilly. There is an objective, ontologically grounded moral order in the light of which responsibility is both recognized and limited. All responsibility is determined on the basis of causality. Of the various senses of responsibility, that fostered by charity is not to be equated with legal or moral responsibility. And finally, no sense of responsibility can engender, as Jaspers would have it, an indelible metaphysical guilt.

Family Matters

Almost eighty-five years ago, philosophers and literary intellectuals as diverse as Edmund Husserl, George Santayana, and Paul Valéry, aware of the declining influence of Christianity, spoke of "the crisis of Western civilization." All three placed their hopes on the revival of the classical sources of Western civilization, with Valéry insisting, in addition, on an acknowledgment of a debt to Roman law and Roman Catholicism. We know that the European Constitution as initially drafted failed to acknowledge both the classical and Christian sources of Western culture. It was subsequently denied approval when put to a popular vote in France and The Netherlands. Redrafted as a treaty, it was eventually passed in 2009 after the intense lobbying of holdouts, Ireland, Poland, and the Czech Republic, by the bureaucracy of Brussels. Husserl and Santayana, even in their prescience, could not have imagined the multicultural diversity that confronts today's secularized Europe, a Europe unable to control its borders or assimilate the flood of immigrants from the Middle East and Africa.

Europe seems to be living off a dying past, perhaps nearing the end of a great culture, not unlike that experienced before the fall of Rome, when internal corruption made possible the barbarian invasions. The decline of morals apart, the birth rate of the native European population alone would attest to decline. The ruling elites of Brussels and the European capitals seem confident that the constitutive elements of what was once called "Christendom" can be maintained without reference to their source. Absent Christianity, Europe has little to defend but its material culture. The fate of a secularized Europe is not without implications for our own country. A few years ago, the highly respected cultural historian, Samuel P. Huntington, published a volume entitled, *Who Are We?* Starting from the premise that the United States once possessed a common core—one may say, an Anglo-Protestant soul—

Huntington believes that sometime between 1920 and 1970 the country lost that soul, succumbing to a liberal virus that has sapped its strength. Eighty years earlier, George Santayana had employed the same metaphor in speaking of Christianity in the West when he wrote: "Our society has lost its soul. The landscape of Christendom is covered with lava: a great eruption and inundation of brute humanity threatens to overwhelm the treasures that artful humanity has created." Huntington is convinced that the United States remains an overwhelmingly Christian nation, yet he is not oblivious to the moral and cultural decline that has weakened the family. He attributes that decline not to gains made by non-Christian religions but to the increased influence of a small but influential number of intellectuals and publicists, atheists and materialists, who in the name of multiculturalism attack the United States, denying its Christian founding and distinctive cultural heritage. In repudiating the inherited, they wish to create a country that does not belong to any civilization, one devoid of a cultural core. They substitute for the rights of individuals the rights of groups, defined largely in terms of race, ethnicity, gender, and sexual preference.

II

I offer the previous observations as background to the topic I have been asked to address this evening. If you are of a certain age, let us say, old enough to be a grandparent, you probably took a number of things for granted. Although your sentiments may have been similar, you might not have said, as did the sister of a newly ordained friend, "I believe in God, my country, and J. Edgar Hoover." Her generation, my generation, took for granted the Church, its teaching, and its sacramental life and rituals. That generation counted on the benefits of a stable government, and without much thought an impartial criminal justice system. I was a part of that generation that understood the value of a stable family life. The divorced tended to be regarded as moral failures and were viewed with suspicion. The wife of Charles de Gaulle, for example, apart from what was required of her in her official life, would not permit a divorced person in her home, so strong was her feeling for the sanctity of marriage. Social policy in my youth was determined by "what is good for the kinder." It was common teaching in my college years that there are two indispensable communities, sometimes called "perfect communities" because they were thought to be self-contained. I am speaking of the state and the family. Both of course required their unity to preserve their very being. That unity was generated by and dependent upon the acknowledgment of a common purpose. The primary purpose of marriage, it was universally recognized, is the procreation and rearing of children. Vatican II changed all that when it unleashed on the Catholic populace a host of ill-trained Catholic theologians who proclaimed a reordering. The primary purpose of marriage, they taught, is self-fulfillment, as if the first precluded the second. Those same theologians were among the first to denounce Paul VI for *Humane Vitae*. And lo and behold, some sought self-fulfillment outside the priesthood. Some were undoubtedly involved in the suppression of the old liturgy which Stuart Reid has called "the greatest act of vandalism in history."

The benefits of family most of us know. A three-generation family is a blessing. I have from childhood delightful memories of Grandpa Schneider and Grandpa Franke. They were not my grandfathers, but that was how they were known in our extended family circle. Grandpa Schneider of German lineage was a member of the family by virtue of the fact that his daughter married one of my uncles; Grandpa Franke of French lineage, by virtue of the fact that his daughter was a high school classmate of my aunt. In memory, I can envisage both as they leaned back in their leather chairs, a cigar in one hand, a glass of brandy in another—well I assume it was brandy, the glass had the shape that I later came to associate with brandy. Children were welcome in both households but advised not to disturb grandfather especially when he was reading his newspaper. Both died in their late eighties; my own grandmother, their contemporary died at age ninety.

To be sure, experience and wisdom come with age, and in a closely knit family members often benefit by deference to the judgment of the elders. But the benefits of family do not await advanced age or even years; they follow closely upon marriage. Within an extended family, surely someone is likely to know about real estate, inheritance, and other taxes, have a pick-up truck, a radial saw, an extension ladder, or other useful tool. That is all masculine stuff, I acknowledge; ladies, on the other hand, have been known to exchange things other than recipes. One or more members of a family are likely to be adept at a musical instrument and can add to the joy of a festive occasion. These are material benefits.

There is also a moral dimension to a family. I once tried to illustrate this in answer to the question, "How do you shield your children from the common culture?" I said something like, keeping television out of the home and added a family slogan, proclaiming in the presence of a distinguished colleague, "Doughertys are different." He held his nose, as if to suggest "they don't bathe." The moral dimension is not reducible to prim and proper behavior, neatness, or even regular attendance at Mass and frequent confession. It may go something like this, "What would your Uncle Henry think if you did something like that," or "Do you think you grandmother would approve," or "Don't disgrace the family," or, simply, "I don't like what I'm seeing."

The importance of what I am calling "family sanction" was recognized by Bishop Otto von Kettler of Mainz, when in the nineteenth century the effects of the industrial revolution were beginning to be felt throughout Europe. Von Kettler, I must explain, is acknowledged to be one of the great social theorists of that day, and his influence on Leo XIII can be discerned in the encyclical *Rerum Novarum*. He was convinced that the businessmen of his native Rhineland, unlike the English, paid a just wage and provided safe working conditions. Marx's theory was inappropriate for Germany. What concerned the Bishop of Mainz was the moral situation that the youth who fled to the cities in search of factory employment were likely to experience. They would be emancipated from the sanctioning or stewarding guidance of their families. An analogous situation today may consist in sending a student off to college.

While still in first or second gear when I leave for work in the morning, I am often delighted in my neighborhood by the sight of parents gathered with their children at one or more of the school bus stops on my usual route. If I am running a bit late, I find many of the mums still there, chatting away. Children help to create a sense of community. The dog walkers are a different breed; they seem a lonely class. I may be reading too much into what I see, but it is undeniable; kids bring people together and often bond them to each other. Think of all those baseball games, soccer games, and transportation hurdles that you endured with other suffering parents; you may find that the empathy created under those circumstances often holds for years.

From the standpoint of social philosophy, the family is viewed as an indispensable instrument for the transmission of morals, tastes, and knowledge; a lawyer might call it "intellectual property." For family traditions to be maintained, it is of vital importance that there is the possibility of transmitting property from one generation to another, personal property to be sure, but what I have in mind is primarily real estate. This was once graphically illustrated for me when in Jerusalem I visited the home of a ninth-generation rabbi. He had the books to prove it; his library, assembled no doubt over those nine generations, extended throughout a rather large house.

Confronted as we are with always newer forms of taking on the part of government, the transmission of material property is always in need of defense. Intellectual inheritance, continuity of standards, and the external forms of civility are achieved only where it is possible to transmit material advantages from one generation to another. Many of the spiritual goods to which I have alluded, are anchored in the material. The family's ability to pass on standards and traditions is closely tied to the possibility of transmitting real estate and other assets. Some argue that each generation should start anew. But it is difficulty to see how the true interest of society would consist in limiting gain to one generation. Where inheritance of property does not exist as in communist countries, men look for other ways of providing for their offspring, such as placing them in positions which might bring them income and prestige that a fortune otherwise would have brought. Inheritance and other taxes can interfere with the cultural transmission of which I am speaking. There is an egalitarian-leveling spirit which ignores this fact. Contrary to the positions of some contemporary philosophers there is no injustice if some people are born to wealthy parents, or are born to kind and intelligent parents. In fact, community is enhanced if some children can start with the advantage that a wealthy home is likely to offer. The same is true if some children inherit greater intelligence than others or are taught better than others at home. Inheritance undeniably confers unmerited advantages on some children, in the sense of inequality. One can concede that liberty may not demand unlimited freedom of bequest. Our point here is that families ought to be free to pass on to their children or to others such possessions as will cause substantial inequality.

There are other issues that in the name of the family we are forced to confront in a secular environment vigorously hostile to the moral teaching of the church. I take it that we are of similar mind in recognizing the evil of contraception, abortion, divorce, stem-cell manipulation, the use of fetal tissue in cosmetics, and the sanctioning of so-called "homosexual marriage," among other issues. We are familiar with the "personally opposed" Catholic politician who declines to defend the Church's teaching on a given subject. Even a well-known, highly regarded prelate capitulated in the days of *Griswold v. Connecticut.* He noted that previous Catholic leaders had opposed any effort to alter laws prohibiting contraception. "But my thinking," he said, "has changed on the matter for the simple reason that I do not see where I have an obligation to impose my religious beliefs on people who just do not accept the same faith as I do." T. S. Eliot would beg to disagree.

The renowned English poet, in an admirable essay first delivered as a broadcast address in February 1937, spoke of the Church's business to interfere in the world. He forcefully opposed the principle of "live and let live." "Some assume," he wrote, "that if the state leaves the Church alone, and to some extent protects it from molestation, then the Church has no right to interfere with the organization of society, or with the conduct of those who deny its beliefs." Addressing the claim that any such interference would be the oppression of the majority by a minority, he reminded his listeners that the Church is not merely for the elect. Whether people say that the Church ought to interfere or whether it ought to mind its own business, depends mostly on whether they agree or disagree with its attitude or judgment upon the issue of the moment. The Church is acclaimed when it supports any cause that is already assured a good deal of secular support. It is attacked, quite naturally, when it opposes anything that people think they want. When there is an occasion for the Church to resist any innovation—either in legislation or in social practice—which is contrary to Christian principles, the Church, says Eliot, must speak. The Church may not always be strong enough to resist successfully, but Eliot insists, "it can never accept as a permanent settlement, one law for itself and another for the world." The Church should not be in any political sense conservative, or liberal, or revolutionary. Conservatism is too often conservation of the wrong things; liberalism always entails a relaxation of discipline, and revolution is a denial of the permanent things. It is much more the business of the Church to say what is wrong—that is, what is inconsistent with Christian doctrine—than to propose particular schemes for improvement. That is the distinctive role of the Church, to say what is always and everywhere wrong. We know from the teaching of Christ that there will always be a tension between church and state, and from our reading of history that a certain tension is desirable. And Eliot makes the point, "When Church and State fall out completely, it is ill with the commonwealth; and when the church and state get along too well there is something wrong with the church."

T. S. Eliot followed his broadcast address with a series of lectures delivered at Corpus Christi College, Cambridge, lectures that were subsequently published as *The Idea of a Christian Society* (Farber and Farber, 1939). Those lectures were premised on a thesis that ran something like this: the current terms in which we discuss international affairs and political theory tend to conceal from us the real issues of contemporary civilization. Eliot was not alone in addressing the oft-forgotten, Christian basis of Western civilization. The cultural historian Christopher Dawson and the French philosopher Jacques Maritain, his contemporaries, were doing so as well. As a matter of fact, Eliot knew their work and acknowledged a debt to both. In common they and many others were disheartened by the secularization of Western civilization, and in common they sensed the tragedy that was about to befall Europe. Within the same year, 1939, Eliot published *The Idea of a Christian Society*, Dawson published *Beyond Politics*, and Maritain submitted to the publisher the manuscript for *Religion and Culture*. In a somewhat different vein, Pius XI promulgated *Casti Connubii*, translated as, "On the Nature and Dignity of Christian Marriage," and Jacques Leclercq, a professor of philosophy at the University of Louvain, Belgium, published *Marriage and the Family*. Whereas Eliot, Dawson, and Maritain in speaking of culture necessarily used large brush strokes appropriate to the cultural historian, the discourse of Pius XI was by contrast "earthy" as he spoke of the family as the on-the-ground bearer of the culture. In antiquity, Aristotle recognized that good states and good households are interconnected.

The Aristotelian Element in Boethius's Understanding of the Trinity

"A person is a supposit of a rational nature." So wrote Boethius fifteen hundred years ago, and that definition has resonated throughout the centuries. Analogously predicated of God, angels, and human beings, Boethius's definition of person remains normative today. In the treatise, *The Trinity is One God, Not Three Gods*, a treatise that we have come to know as *de Trinitate*, Boethius opens with this sentence: "I have long pondered this problem with such mind as I have and all the light God has lent me."[1] For Boethius, to embrace the Catholic faith is not to leap into the dark. The Church from its early centuries has consistently taught the reasonableness of belief, has taught that Christ came in the fullness of time when the intellect of the West was prepared to receive the truths of the Gospel. The early Church Fathers brought to their study of Scripture the language of Athens, the categories of Aristotle, and the teachings of Plato and of the Stoa. Many of the early fathers, among them St. Basil and the two Gregories, studied at Athens. Marius Victorinus (ca. A.D. 280–365), sometimes called "the Augustine before Augustine," was similarly schooled and is considered the first Latin Father to compose a systematic metaphysical treatise on the Trinity. He may have been the first to speak of God as "pure act of *to be*." He was convinced that scriptural statements about the equality and the distinction of Father, Son, and Holy Ghost can be reconciled but only if one does not make philosophical mistakes like Basil of Ancyra. To the philosopher, Justin Martyr, a convert to Christianity in A.D. 130 and a martyr during the reign of Prefect Junius Rusticus (163–167 A.D.), Greek philosophy and Christianity appeared as one and the same divine revelation. For Justin, Christianity absorbed philosophy, not the other way round. "Whatever things were rightly said among men," he writes, "are the property of Christians." Philosophers may partly share in the *Logos*, but Christians partake of the whole.

Boethius in his day will echo the outlook of Justin and Victorinus. Philosophy may be productive of wisdom, but a deeper wisdom is offered to the Christian. To make that wisdom one's own, one has to integrate it to what is known of the natural order. Whatever is inherited becomes our own only if in appropriating it we transform it so that it becomes an intellectual *habitus*, part of ourselves. It is not what is inherited that counts but what a person makes of it. Clearly Boethius made the most of what he inherited and set about making sure that inheritance would be available to yet another generation. His ambition to translate all the known works of Plato and Aristotle was cut short with his execution in 524 A.D.

Boethius, we know from subsequent events, stood at a watershed in the history of the West. He was aware that the world in which he had grown to manhood was doomed and that the world coming into being was not his own. He was not alone in that judgment. The *Imperium Romanum* had come to an end with Alaric's conquest of the city of Rome in 410. In the aftermath of the barbarian invasions of the western part of the Roman Empire in the late fifth and early sixth centuries, cultural life had declined, and the future of the empire was unclear. Rome was no longer the symbol of world order. The Greek literary tradition had all but died, and the Hellenism that well served the Fathers of the Church was losing its hold.

Boethius was one of a few in the upper classes who saw the importance of preserving an inherited literary culture, and he set about transmitting the texts of ancient philosophy to posterity. It was his ambition not only to make available to his countrymen the works of Plato and Aristotle but to show the compatibility of the two, often interpreting Aristotle through the eyes of Plato. Cassiodorus (ca. 490–585), a younger contemporary and author of the oldest biography of Boethius, also understood the value of Greek learning and, upon founding a Benedictine monastery on his family's property at Squillaca, far from a decadent Rome on the Adriatic in southern Italy, set about having his monks copy ancient texts.

Parenthetically, one may note that our present somewhat resembles that ancient past. In our own country and in much of Europe, education at all levels has lost contact with the classics that heretofore provided the core of a liberal education. The value of classical learning was never contested by leading philosophers of the twentieth century, yet our universities have all but abandoned the Western literary cannon. To read Husserl, Heidegger, and Gadamer, for example, is to appreciate their indebtedness to the Greeks. George Santayana, the Spanish-born American philosopher, eschewing the pragmatism of his mentor William James, thought of his own work as a restatement of Aristotle's metaphysics.

It is to be remembered that the Aristotelian corpus was not fully available in the West until the advent of the thirteenth century. Boethius had access to the *Organon*, that is, the logical works of Aristotle, but not the *de Anima*, the *Physics* or the *Metaphysics*. Yet we find elements of the natural philosophy of Aristotle throughout his writing. Distinguishing between faith and reason, Boethius describes philosophy as an effort to understand and to explain the world of nature around us. The role of theology is to explain the doctrines delivered through revelation, but theology must draw upon the categories of being. Sorting and classifying, he first distinguishes between faith and theology, and in an effort to locate theology within the sciences, he further distinguishes three levels of scientific abstraction, that of physics, of mathematics, and of theology, a classification that St. Thomas is to elucidate further in Books Four and Five of his *Commentary on the de Trinitate*.

Throughout the *Theological Tractates* and the *Consolation of Philosophy*, Boethius draws heavily on Aristotelian notions of substance, matter, form, and the incorporeal in order to show that in Christ the divine nature and the human nature are real and really distinct. He makes full use of Aristotle's categories in speaking of God as a "substance" but not as a substance in the usual sense—i.e., as a subject of accidental properties. Having previously made the distinction between the corporeal and the incorporeal, he finds that man by virtue of his immaterial soul transcends the merely corporeal, and he goes on to show how predicates normally said of man can be analogically predicated of God: predicates such as greatness, simplicity, omniscience, goodness, and justice. From his study of the *Organon*, he appropriates the distinction between substance and accident, between matter and form, soul and body, and, by implication, essence and existence. From his study of Plato, he incorporates Plato's theory of forms and his doctrine of participation. We have studies highlighting the Platonic heritage of Thomism. Even more pronounced is the Platonic element in the philosophy of Boethius, yet he remains fundamentally an Aristotelian.

I should have said at the beginning that this paper does not promise anything new. There are scholars who have spent years explicating the work of Boethius, and I am not about to sort out the controversies involving the interpretation of his texts. This is foremost an appreciation of the time-transcending character of his work, but not merely that. Boethius holds interest for us because in many ways we are in a similar position. When the Greek literary tradition was losing its hold at the end of the sixth century, Boethius sensed that a loss of the Hellenic tradition was not in the best interest of Christianity. The tools he needed to understand the Catholic faith were those provided by Aristotle and Plato, and he brought them into service as he attempted to understand the Trinity, the Incarnation, and other mysteries related to the faith. Although occupied in theological reflection, he regarded himself as engaged in the same activity as were Plato and Aristotle, the search for truth about nature and human nature, a philosophical search now complemented by revelation. There is no need to reconcile reason and faith; they are but two movements in one and the same enterprise. It is the scholar's duty to first study the real nature of anything before he formulates a belief about it. Thus, when discussing the mystery of the Trinity in an attempt to understand how three persons can exist in one God, Boethius first discusses from a philosophical perspective the marks of unity and difference. Men differ neither by genus nor by species but by their accidents. The fact that Father, Son, and Holy Spirit are one is because of the absence of difference with respect to essence. Where there is no difference, there is no sort of plurality according to number. God is nothing other than His own essence. When we say "God is just," we are not mentioning an accidental quality, but rather a substantial one. Similarly, God's being and goodness are one and the same.

In the *Consolation*, we find discussions of the principles of identity, (a thing must preserve its unity to preserve its very being), intelligibility

(intelligibility follows degrees of being: to the extent that a thing exists, it is intelligible), and finality (God rules the universe by the helm of his goodness).[2] The *Theological Tractates* produce a slew of distinctions and axioms that are carried in the scholastic tradition through the centuries. In the *de Trinitate* and the other explicitly theological writings, such as the *Letters to John the Deacon, de Fide Catholica*, and *Contra Eutychen*, we find a doctrine of the hierarchy of being and a doctrine of participation and their various formulations. We are told that to the extent a thing exists, it is intelligible. And its corollary: intelligibility follows participation, for the existence of the imperfect in any order whatsoever presupposes the perfect. Being and unity are convertible terms; so, too, being and the good. To maintain itself in being, a thing must maintain its unity. This passage, after a series of distinctions, leads Boethius to his famous definition of person. "Nature," he begins, "belongs to those things, which since they exist, can in some measure be apprehended by the mind."[3] What then is a nature? Although a nature can be considered abstractly and predicated of many as a universal, a nature can have substantial existence only as a particular. Nature can be predicated of all substances, corporeal or incorporeal. A corporeal nature is further identified as "either that which can act or that which can be acted upon, (for) the power to act and suffer belongs to all corporeals, and to the soul of all corporeals; for the soul both acts in the body and suffers by the body."[4] Speaking of corporeal substances, some are living, some are not. Of living substances, some are sensitive, others insensitive; of sensitive substances, some are rational, some irrational. Of rational substances, there is only one that is immutable and impassible by nature, namely, God.[5] All this, step by step, leading up to a definition of person: "A person is an individual substance of a rational nature."[6]

With reason, Boethius has been called the last of the Roman philosophers and the first of the scholastic theologians. I would say scholastic philosophers. The essence of scholasticism is its conviction that philosophy is a science capable of reaching conclusions that can be passed from one generation to another. Its empirical character is established by its care to distinguish and to define. As Boethius, following the logic of Aristotle, clearly saw, a definition is not a description of the accidental features of a substance but a rendering of the intelligible nature under consideration. It is that defining operation that securely anchors thought in the natural order and gives it its empirical character. One schooled in the scholastic tradition is not only convinced that nature is intelligible but that one can reason from effect to cause, rendering intelligible that which is not intelligible in itself. This confidence in method gives one the confidence that there is a body of truth that can be passed from one generation to another. This conviction supports our respect for classical learning. Just as one does not have to rediscover the elements of the periodic table, one does not have to start all over again when one begins to reflect on God, human nature and self-fulfillment. Sadly, the Church in an attempt to engage the modern world in the aftermath of Vatican II, gave up much when it abandoned scholastic philosophy and with it the Greek and Latin requirement that formed part of the core curriculum in many of its institutions. Still, Boethius is there to remind us of loss and of the need to recover and perpetuate a valuable legacy.

Benedict on the Nature of Scientific Enquiry

There is a short passage in Pope Benedict XVI's recently published *Jesus of Nazareth* that deserves an appreciative philosophical comment. That is the passage in the Foreword, wherein Benedict addresses the status of biblical exegesis and briefly discusses the nature of scientific enquiry. Philosophers of science struggle with the issue of objectivity and even ask whether truth is possible in natural science, let alone, the much more difficult terrain of the social sciences, of history, and of what we have come to call "the sciences of man." The issues addressed are vexing to even the most seasoned philosophers of science. To what extent in any enquiry is objectivity possible? Or to put the question another way, what are the constraints that introduce uncertainty into any investigation?

Biblical exegesis partakes of the nature of history and is subject to all the constraints associated with that discipline. It is understood that modern biblical exegetes come to their subject using contemporary historical methods to reconstruct biblical accounts of events from *Genesis* to the *Acts of the Apostles*. In approaching their texts, consciously or not, they often come with preconceived notions that inevitably blur their vision. Benedict reminds us that, "already during Jesus' lifetime, people tried to interpret this mysterious figure by applying to him categories that were familiar to them and that were considered apt for deciphering his mystery."[1] Disputing the reliability of ancient texts relating to Christ, some modern exegetes have raised doubts even about the existence of Jesus, drawing a distinction between Jesus as reconstructed through historical methods and the Christ of faith as understood through a theological tradition. Still other scholars ask to what extent the motivation of the Evangelists shaped the Gospel accounts, asking what sources were available to them as they wrote, asking how soon after the events they described did the Evangelists produce their accounts, all factors that could lead to inaccuracies, exaggerations or inventions. Given the myriad pictures of Christ that have emerged over the past half-century, Benedict finds it necessary to restate the obvious. Jesus of the Gospels is without doubt the real "historical Jesus." The biblical Jesus "is much more logical, and historically speaking, much more intelligible than the reconstructions we have been presented with in the last decades."[2] Furthermore, the Gospel accounts are accessible to all, the unlearned as well as the learned.

Why is it necessary to reaffirm what the layman takes to be obvious, namely that Jesus of the Gospels is the real historical Jesus? The answer is to be found in part because of the following achieved by some scholars, who, in working from a purely materialistic or agnostic perspective, have cast doubt on the divinity of Christ. David Friedrich Strauss (1808–1874), though not the first, is a prime example of the scholar who deliberately attempted to undermine Christianity in the interest of replacing it with a "scientific materialism." His two-volume *Das Leben Jesu* (1835–36) presented the Gospels as a collection of historical myths, the unintentionally created legendary embodiments of primitive Christianity's popular hopes. That work was to have considerable influence on nineteenth- and twentieth-century liberal Protestantism, to which some Catholic scholars were not immune, insofar as they too began to distinguish between the "historical Jesus" and "Christ of the Gospels." Rudolf Bultmann, following the lead of Strauss, became one of the most influential Protestant theologians of the twentieth century. Bultmann's *History of the Synoptic Tradition* (1921) seemed to provide highly scientific arguments that deprived the Synoptic Gospels, that is, the Gospels of Matthew, Mark, and Luke, of all historical truth, leaving Jesus of Nazareth as a deluded Jew who lived, preached, and died in Palestine, but who never worked miracles or rose from the dead except in the imagination of his followers.

As far back as 1890, competent Catholic scholars had begun to investigate the archeological background and the literary forms employed by the Scriptures. Pope Leo XIII, aware of contemporary trends in biblical scholarship, established in 1902 the Pontifical Biblical Commission with a mandate to study new methodologies and to evaluate the resulting biblical erudition, but at the same time he wanted the Commission to safeguard the faith against unwarranted interpretations of the Bible. In his words the Commission was founded in order that the texts of Sacred Scripture "will find here and from every quarter the most thorough interpretation demanded by our times and be shielded, not only from every breath of error, but also from every temerarious opinion." It was also the wish of Leo XIII that a periodical bulletin of biblical studies be published at Rome. In 1904 Pius X empowered the Commission to confer the degrees of Licentiate and Doctor in the faculty of Sacred Scripture on priests who, having attained the doctorate in theology, had also passed the relevant examinations established by the Commission. At about the same time, Pere Marie-Joseph Lagrange, O.P., an early promoter of method exegesis, founded L'École Pratique d'études biblique in Jerusalem. In 1943 Pope Pius XII issued the encyclical *Divino Afflante Spiritu* that Catholic scholars embraced as a kind of Magna Carta, freeing them to pursue biblical studies without the constraints that had previously bound them to tradition.

Carroll Stuhmueller, C.P., tells us that scriptural investigation subsequently drew Catholic and Protestant scholars together in a common study of the Bible. In this enterprise each could lay aside dogmatic differences that had divided Christendom for four hundred years and go back to centuries earlier, to the pre-theological days of apostolic Christianity, to the days when the scriptures were first prepared and written down.[3] He goes on to suggest that biblical scholars were in effect clearing the ground and turning the soil for the future ecumenical council.

Bultmann's influence continues within the halls of biblical scholarship, where the spirit of "form criticism" yet prevails. Many of his opinions have acquired the status of dogma, in spite of the fact that much of his work is not the result of historical findings but the consequence of a set of systematic presuppositions. Bultmann was convinced that the essential message of the Gospels could be and should be disengaged from the mythical context in which they were written. To that end he went about this by reinterpreting the myths of the virgin birth, the Incarnation and the Resurrection in the language of Heidegger and 20th-century existentialism. Christian faith, he taught, should be comparatively uninterested in the "historical Jesus" and concentrate on the time-transcendent teaching of the Church as grounded in John and the Pauline epistles.

Given the tendency of form criticism to undermine the faith in its search for the "historical Jesus," Benedict calls attention to the limits of the historical critical method. As a historical method, its object is specific, the time framework in which the texts originated. As Benedict notes, "It attempts to identify and understand the past—as it was in itself—with the greatest possible precision, in order then to find out what the author could have said and intended to say in the context of the mentality and events of the time." He adds "To the extent that it remains true to itself, the historical method not only has to investigate the biblical word as a thing in the past, but also it has to let it remain in the past."[4] We cannot bring the past to the present. Words spoken in the past may have a meaning for today, but the object of biblical exegesis is not contemporary relevance.

From the vantage point of the philosophy of science, history is not a science. Demonstration eludes it. In our efforts to know the past we can never go beyond the domain of hypothesis. An hypothesis, by definition, is a plausible explanation for a datum encountered in experience, in the case of history, surviving literary texts, perhaps some uncovered by recent archeological research and a general knowledge of the period in which an event occurred. Some hypotheses offered to explain a particular event or offered as an aid in understanding a particular period may enjoy a higher degree of certainty than others. Biblical exegetes may speak of "the scientific tools of modern historical research" or of the historical Jesus as a "scientific construct" prescinding from what Christian faith or later Church teaching says about Jesus. Still the historian must remain conscious of the limits of his "certainties." There cannot be historical knowledge without recreation of the past by a knower, a knowing subject. Whatever is written is written from a point of view. A scholar cannot approach his texts or period of investigation without some degree of empathy for the object of his study, a feeling that enables him to find his way into the past, enabling him to grasp it, as it were, from within. This process results in a fusion of objectivity and subject. It is not a matter of indifference whether a person says, "All history goes to Christ and come from

Him." Prominent philosophers of science, we might add, are much more circumspect in their claims to objectivity than some biblical exegetes.

Benedict reminds us that a canonical reading of Sacred Scripture requires the reader to keep in mind the whole of the Bible. Through the Scriptures "a voice greater than man" is speaking, and that voice has to be treated as such. Individual texts read in the context of Scripture as a whole exhibit an internal unity that renders intelligible words that cannot be taken as human words when their author is Christ Himself. Benedict says of his own work, "Of course, I take for granted everything the Council and modern exegesis tells us about literary genres, about authorial intention, and about the fact that the Gospels were written in the context and speak within the living milieu of communities." He states humbly that his Jesus of Nazareth is solely an expression of his personal research and not an exercise of his magisterial office. "Everyone is free, then, to contradict me."[5]

In evaluating an inquiry, the subjective cannot be ignored. Biblical exegetes bring to their study their personal dispositions. Anyone who has had the opportunity to study with or listen to a spectrum of contemporary biblical scholars recognizes that the early training of the exegete colors his findings. The *habitus* of the historian is not that of the philosopher. The two may not contradict each other, but their emphasis differs. We see this early on in Marius Victorinus (ca. 280–365), who was tutored by Polycarp, who had learned of the life and teachings of Christ from the Apostle John himself. Victorinus, steeped in the classical learning of his day, became perhaps the first to speak of God as having revealed himself in the language of *being*.

From the vantage point of the philosophy of science, Benedict is on solid ground in questioning the objectivity of those historians who come to their material with certain ideological commitments. In the natural sciences, it is taken for granted that the scientist is focused on the objective and real inner workings of nature. Yet all science is partially a social construct. Reaching a consensus even in the natural sciences is a complex social process in which empirical evidence is only a part. Consensus among scientists on a particular scientific perspective arises out of both social interactions among members of a scientific community and interactions with the world. How much more so is this true of history and of the social sciences where interpretation is even more pronounced. The process of writing history is so infused with all sorts of human values and judgments that what ends up being proclaimed to be historical fact may bear little resemblance to the actual event or period. Reality is no doubt capable of sustaining more than one account, but investigators often see what is in their personal interest to see. David Friedrich Strauss's *Das Leben Jesu* is a case in point. Strauss, working from the perspective of a "scientific materialist," could not, because of his philosophical position, accept the literal truth of the miracles recounted in the New Testament and, of course, could not accept the divinity of Christ. Bultmann provides another example insofar as he assumes the unreliability of the biblical account, even as he attempts to salvage the message (*kerygma*) of the Gospels by recasting them in Heideggerian terms.

One has to admire the frankness of the scholar who concludes a decades-long study, acknowledging that to the best of his ability he has tried to incorporate all that the Council and modern exegesis has produced, and yet proclaims simply, "I trust the Gospels." Benedict writes, "Unless there had been something extraordinary in what happened, unless the person and words of Jesus radically surpasses the hopes and expectations of the time, there is no way to explain why he was crucified or made such an impact."[6]

Moderate Islam

A moderate Islam is undoubtedly the dream of many Westernized Muslims, Middle East diplomats, and businessmen, let alone the rest of us who receive daily reports of suicide bombings in the Middle East. We are told time and again by Islamic apologists that Islam is a peaceful religion. University and commercial presses flood the book market with studies that present Islam as one of three "Abrahamic faiths," deserving of the same respect accorded to Christianity and Judaism, its doctrine and history notwithstanding. Many of the Islamic studies favored by university presses are apologetic in tone, cosmetic treatises produced in the wake of 9/11 to show that Islam is not the fanatical religion we take it to be despite the suicide bombings that have horrified the West. There are exceptions of course. Harvard University Press published Bernard Lewis's semicritical, *What Went Wrong?: The Clash Between Islam and Modernity in the Middle East* (2002),[1] and more recently, the University of Chicago Press has released Rémi Brague's historical study, *The Legend of the Middle Ages*.[2] Given the challenge facing Europe, and to a lesser extent North America—challenges resulting from an influx of Muslim immigrants who refuse assimilation and demand the right to live under their own law within the host country—it is incumbent on those who value their own traditions to become better acquainted with the newcomers. Many readers may have grown up with the "melting pot" image that was once meaningful when immigrants to the United States were mostly of European origin. That image is frequently invoked to suggest that we have nothing to fear from a massive influx of immigrants from other cultures. The truth is that Europeans who entered North America in the nineteenth century may have come from different nations and spoken different languages but nevertheless possessed common cultural roots. Since the 1960s U.S. immigration policy has favored those of non-European origin. The favored newcomers have their origins not in what used to be known as Christendom but in the Middle East, northern Africa, and parts of Asia.

A large majority seemingly have no intent to assimilate Western ways and use U.S. law to secure exceptions from the common law in support of their traditional ways of life.

To get an unbiased account of Islam, there is no better place to start than Ignaz Goldziher's *Introduction to Islamic Theology and Law*.[3] The book has an interesting history. Responding to an invitation in 1906 to deliver a series of lectures in the United States, Goldziher wrote the lectures in German, but for reasons of health and his inability to secure a reliable English translation, never made the trans-Atlantic voyage to deliver them. A German edition was published in 1910, but a satisfactory English translation was not available until 1981 when Princeton University Press issued a translation by Andras and Ruth Hamori. Bernard Lewis provides the introduction. Goldziher, Lewis tells the reader, was a Hungarian Jew by birth and by virtue of interest and linguistic ability became a respected "orientalist," as Middle East scholars were called in the Vienna of his day. In the judgment of Lewis, as a guide to Muslim faith, law, doctrines, and devotions, Goldziher "was much better placed than his Christian compatriots to study Islam and to understand the Muslims. To know rabbinic law and submit to its rules make it easier to understand the Holy Law of Islam and those who obey it." Rémi Brague, whose work we will consider momentarily, similarly praises Goldziher as "perhaps the greatest student of Islam who ever lived."[4]

Goldziher begins his account of the origins of Islam by contrasting the long-suffering ascetic of Mecca with the Warrior Prophet of Medina. At Mecca, the Prophet's message was an eclectic composite of religious ideas and regulations. "It was with borrowed blocks," writes Goldziher, "that Mohammed built his eschatological message. He did not proclaim any new ideas, nor did he enrich earlier conceptions of man's relations to the transcendent and the infinite." The revelations Mohammed proclaimed in Mecca, Goldziher maintains, did not establish a new religion but instead created a pious mood that found expression in ascetic practices that could also be found among Jews and Christians of the period, i.e., in devotions (recitations with genuflections and prostrations), voluntary privations (fasting), and acts of charity (alms-giving). It was only after Mohammed and his followers were forced to leave Mecca and settle in Medina that Islam in 622 came into being. In Medina the long-suffering ascetic was transformed into a warrior, a conqueror, and a statesman. Goldziher suggests the move to Medina was in some ways detrimental to Mohammed's character. Not long after arriving in Medina, Mohammed, to oblige his growing number of followers, gave approval to armed raids against Meccan caravans that passed near Medina on their way to Syria. War and victory soon became the means and end of his prophetic vocation. Whereas he had formerly disdained earthly possessions, he now set about regulating the distribution of plunder and fixing laws of inheritance and property. Other changes in outlook took place. Whereas early passages of the Qur'an acknowledge as true places of worship monasteries, churches, and synagogues, in the Medina revelations Mohammed attacks his original teachers, the Christian monks and the Jewish scholars of scripture. Polemics against Jews and Christians, in fact, occupy a large part of the Medina revelations. Mohammed now places himself at the end of a chain of prophets, demanding recognition as the renewer of Abraham's religion, as its restorer from distortion and decay. The triumphs that the Prophet and his companions soon gained against their adversaries served to strengthen belief in him and his mission among his followers.

Clearly, Islam did not enter the world as a fully formed system. The unfolding of Islamic thought, the fixing of the modalities of Islamic practice, and the establishment of Islamic institutions became the work of future generations. The religious congregation of Mecca was transformed in Medina into a rudimentary political structure, one might say, on its way to becoming a world empire. With conquest, the basis of the administration of state had to be laid. The codification of Islamic law thus took precedence over the development of an Islamic theology. Continued war and increasing conquests demanded the establishment of legal criteria for the conduct of war and for statutes to deal with the conquered peoples. Statutes were needed to clarify the position of subject peoples in the state and to regulate the economic situation created by the taking of spoils. Peace treaties granted to the subjected Christians of the Byzantine Empire, for example, allowed Christians to practice their religion but with some restrictions on its public manifestation, in exchange for the payment of a "toleration tax."[5] The word "Islam," Goldziher reminds his reader, means submission. "The word expresses first and foremost a feeling of dependency on an unbounded omnipotence to which man must submit and resign his will." Submission is the dominant principle inherent in all manifestations of Islam: in its ideas, forms, ethics, and worship, and, of course, demanded of conquered peoples. Adherence to Islam means not only an act of actual or theoretical submission to a political system but requires the acceptance of certain articles of faith. Therein lies a difficulty.

The Prophet cannot be called a theologian. The development of a theology was necessarily the work of subsequent generations. Islam does not have the doctrinal uniformity of a church. Its history and inner dynamics, Goldziher shows, are characterized by the assimilation of foreign influences. He speaks of the dogmatic development of Islam under the influence of Hellenistic thought, the indebtedness of Islam to Persian political ideas, and the contribution of neo-Platonism and Hinduism to Islamic mysticism. As time passed, a new set of texts developed alongside the Qur'an. First-hand accounts of Mohammed's words and actions became the narrative known as *sunna*. Traceable to the days of the Prophet, through a chain of reliable authorities who handed down pertinent information from generation to generation, the *sunna* are given textual expression in the *hadith*, which show what the Companions, with the Prophet's approval, held to be exclusively correct. As such they serve as a norm for practical judgment.[6]

It became the vocation of the Islamic theologian to interpret the *hadith*, but not only that; his became the arduous task of deriving from the Qur'an a system of beliefs that are coherent, self-sufficient and free of self-contradictions. "For the Prophet's beliefs," Goldziher explains, "were reflected in his soul in shades that varied with the moods that dominated him. In consequence it was not long before a harmonizing theology had to assume the task of solving theoretical problems such conditions caused."[7] Once a holy writ had become established, there emerged around those formally defined texts a tangle of dogmatic commentaries. The commentaries provided an inexhaustible source from which the speculations of systematic theology subsequently flowed.

Given that theologians dispute with theologians, sects were inevitable. In chapter-length treatises, Goldziher explores the development of Sunni and Shiite Islam and similarly devotes considerable attention to asceticism and Sufism. His narrative ends by his taking notice of a promising Pan-Muslim movement and the Congress of Kazan, where in August 1906 it was resolved that a single textbook could be used for Sunnis and Shiites and that teachers could be chosen indifferently from both sects. The hope for a Pan-Arab movement has faded. If anything, the difference between Shiite and Sunni has come more pronounced in the aftermath of the Iran-Iraq War (1980–88).

One hundred years and decades of scholarship later, the "orientalist" of times past is now apt to be recognized as a professor of Middle East or Islamic Studies. Rémi Brague, one of the most important contemporary French scholars, bears an even more specialized title at the University of Paris, "Professor of Arabic Medieval Philosophy." The premise that animates his latest study, *The Legend of the Middle Ages: Philosophical Explorations of Medieval Christianity, Judaism and Islam,* is that the Middle Ages is a period of history that has something to tell us about ourselves. He does not discuss the origins of Islam, but focuses on its medieval development, especially at the hands of the medieval Arabic philosophers. Addressing the genesis of European culture Brague acknowledges, "Europe borrowed its nourishment, first from the Greco-Roman world that preceded it, then from the world of Arabic culture that developed in parallel with it, and finally from the Byzantine world. It is from the Arab world, in particular, that Europe gained the texts of Aristotle, Galen, and many others, once translated from the Arabic into Latin, fed the twelfth century renaissance. Later the Byzantine world provided the original version of those same texts, which permitted close study and alimented the flowering of Scholasticism." Where would Thomas Aquinas have been, he asks, if he had not found a worthy adversary in Averroes? What would Duns Scotus have contributed if he had not taken Avicenna as a point of departure?

Brague provides a set of distinctions rarely encountered in contemporary literature, i.e., between theology in Christianity and Kalam in Islam, between philosophy in Christianity and falsafa in Islam, elaborating on the terms and the difference in understanding they make.

Islamic philosophy is usually seen as beginning with al-Kindi around the ninth century and ending with Averroes around the twelfth century. No one contests the fact that Muslims continued to think after Averroes, but what remains to be defined is to what extent that thought can be called "philosophy." There are in history highly respectable works that one would never call philosophical but which we would nevertheless describe as "wisdom literature" or "thoughts." Heidegger, Brague tells us, would place "thought" on a higher plane than philosophy. Brague is particularly sensitive to the broader cultural context in which philosophy is developed. He finds that the opinions generally admitted within a given community provide the basis on which philosophy is built. Those opinions are historically conditioned, and they come in the final analysis, he maintains, from the legislator of the community. All medieval works were affected by this phenomenon. Within Christianity, revelation is the all-important communal bond. Muslim and Jewish revelations, which are presented as laws, do not pose the same problems as Christian revelation. Reconciling religion and philosophy is an epistemological problem in Christianity and may even be a psychological one, but in Islam and Judaism reconciling religion and revelation is a political problem. Unlike Islam and Judaism, Christianity includes the Magisterium of the Church whose teaching is granted authority in the intellectual domain.

The institutionalization of philosophy, Brague points out, took place under the tutelage of the Church and remains exclusively European. There was indeed something like higher education in all three Mediterranean worlds, but the teaching of philosophy at the university level existed neither in the Muslim world nor in Jewish communities. Jewish philosophy and Muslim philosophy were private enterprises. It is usual to compare the great philosophers of each tradition, for example, Averroes, Maimonides, and Thomas Aquinas, but the difference is that Thomas was one of many engaged in the same corporate activity, standing out it is true among countless obscure figures. Within Islam there is no corpus of canonical texts that lend themselves to *disputatio*. To illustrate the difference, Brague remarks, "You can be a perfectly competent rabbi or imam without ever having studied philosophy. In contrast, a philosophical background is a necessary part of the basic equipment of the Christian theologian." Leo Strauss, acknowledging the status of philosophy in Christianity, on the one hand, and Islam and Judaism, on the other, regards the institutionalization of philosophy in the Christian world as a double-edged sword. The official acknowledgment of philosophy in the Christian world made philosophy subject to ecclesiastical supervision, whereas the precarious position of philosophy in the Islamic-Jewish world guaranteed its private character and therewith its inner freedom from supervision. Brague contests Strauss on this point, as would any Catholic scholar who has pursued a philosophical vocation.

Brague offers an interesting treatment of the difference between Christianity and Islam from the Muslim point of view. Ibn Khaldun (1332–1406) he takes as an authoritative source. In Ibn Khaldun's view, as presented by Brague, within the Muslim community the holy war is a religious duty because of the universal character of the Muslim mission and the obligation to convert all non-Muslims to Islam either by persuasion or by force. In consequence the caliphate and royal authority are rightly united in Islam so that the person in charge can devote his available strength to both objectives at the same time. "The other religious groups," Ibn Khaldun believes, "do not have a universal mission and the holy war is not a religious duty to them, save only for purposes of defense. It has thus come about that the person in charge of religious affairs in other religious groups is not concerned with power politics. Royal authority comes to those who have it by accident, and in some way that has nothing to do with religion and not because they are under obligation to gain power over other nations." Holy war exists only within Islam and furthermore, Ibn Khaldun insists, is imposed by Sharia.

Its theological warrant aside, Brague asks how jihad is viewed from the vantage point of Islam's greatest philosophers. He puts the question to three Aristotelians, al Farabi, Avicenna, and Averroes, all of whom profess belief in Islam. All three permit the waging of holy war against those who refuse Islam, al Farabi and Averroes against the Christians, Avicenna again the pagans of his native Persia. Al Farabi, who lived and wrote in the lands where the enemy was the Byzantine empire, draws up a list of seven justifications for war, including the right to conduct war in order to acquire something the state desires but is in possession of another, the right of combat against people for whom it would be better if they served but who refuse the yoke of slavery, and the right to wage holy war to force people to accept what is better for them if they do not recognize it spontaneously. Averroes, writing in the farthest western part of the Islamic empire, approves without reservation the slaughter of dissidents, calling for the elimination of a people whose continued existence might harm the state. Avicenna condones conquest and readily grants to the leader of his ideal society the right to annihilate those who are called to truth but reject it. In general the philosophers express no remorse about the widespread bloodletting, and Brague offers some additional examples. Al Farabi has nothing to say against the murder of "bestial" men. Avicenna suggests that the religious skeptic should be tortured until he admits the difference between the true and the not true and is penitent. Averroes advocates the elimination of the mentally handicapped. In the final chapter of *The Legend of the Middle Ages*, Brague asks, "Was Averroes a good guy?" Yes, in spite of the fact that he condoned the extermination of the handicapped, favored the execution of heretics, and sanctioned what today is called ethnic cleansing. Thomas Aquinas accused him of being more the corrupter of Aristotelian philosophy than its interpreter.

Those who insist that Islam is a peaceful religion are either woefully ignorant of its history or willfully suppress a lot of textual evidence to the contrary. Ali A. Allawi, who has served in as a Minister in several postwar Iraq governments, is neither. His recent book, *The Crisis of Islamic Civilization*, is his attempt to understand Islam's medieval past in the light of the future.[8] He tells his reader that the book is "one person's attempt to understand the factors behind the spiritual decay of Islam and what the future holds if this process is not halted or reversed." The book focuses not on Islam from its founding or on historical Islam, but on Islam of the last two hundred years, from the early nineteenth century when Western imperialism forced an encounter with modernity for which Islam was not prepared.

Allawi approaches his topic with a description of the Iraq of his youth, the Iraq of the 1950s, a period in which the ruling class and cultural and intellectual elites had moved away from an overt identification with Islam. "Islam," he writes, "was not a noticeable factor in daily life. Religion was mandatory in school . . . (but) nobody taught us the rules of prayer or expected us to fast in Ramadan. . . . Women, not only in my own family but throughout the urban middle class, wore only Western clothes." The only connection with a pre-modern past, he relates, was that his grandfather always wore the "distinguishing and dignified dress of robes and turbans of an old-line merchant." Allawi continues, "I don't recall ever coming across the word 'jihad' in any contemporary context. The prevailing rhetoric had more to do with Arab destiny and anti-imperialism." Secularism, he tells us, had the Muslim world by the throat. "Modernity was flooding in everywhere and people seemed to want more of it, cinemas and snack bars, cabarets and country clubs, freely flowing alcohol and mixed parties. Baghdad was turning into Babylon, its hedonistic predecessor of yore. And it was not much different . . . in Casablanca, Cairo, Damascus, Istanbul, Tehran, Karachi and Jakarta."

But the cultural climate began to change in the 1960s and not simply because of ascendant military dictatorships throughout much of the Muslim world. Almost imperceptibly, there had begun a re-spiritualization of Islam. The period called for reflection. The Muslim world was confronted with the fading of its own civilization, increasing indifference, and outright abandonment of the foundational and spiritual basis of the faith. By the end of the 1970s, spiritual Islam as a way of worship became eclipsed by a resurgent militant, political, and violent Islam that increasingly seemed to define Islam in the eyes of the West. In Allawi's judgment, "political Islam" is but a manifestation of an ailment rather than the ailment itself. Sectarian, ethnic, and racial hatreds continuously trump the ideals of Islamic unity. "The murderous violence unleashed by Wahhabi-inspired Islamists was accompanied by laborious jurisprudential 'justifications.'"

Allawi goes on to say that while Muslims may have a common political culture and share other affinities, there is no political unity among them. The idea of a pan-Islamic political unity is as chimerical as a union, let us say, of the English-speaking world. In spite of ideological unity at one level, the natural state of Islam is diversity, "tribal," it could be said, given the broad range of sects and groups within it. Yet in Allawi's judgment, given the power blocs confronting Islam—namely, the United States, a mercantilist China, and an expanding European Union—Muslim countries may have to forge a power bloc unique to themselves in the financial sector to bypass the Breton Woods institutions such as the World Bank and the International Monetary Fund. The latter, he thinks, along with the World Trade Organization, are largely subservient to the interests of Western powers.

In explaining the title of the book, Allawi writes, "The crisis of Islamic civilization arises from the fact that it has been thwarted from demarcating its own pathways into contemporary life. The Western world of modernity has been superimposed on its own world view, and Islam has been unable to relate to the modern world except through this awkward and painfully alien framework." Allawi rejects Samuel P. Huntington's thesis in *A Clash of Civilizations,*[9] wherein Huntington speaks of the confrontation of Islam and Christianity. The "clash," as Allawi sees it, is between the secular materialist culture of the West and the spiritual culture of Islam. He warns, "If Muslims want the very things that modern technological civilization promises . . . they will have to acknowledge the roots of that civilization in order to become an active and creative part of it. Otherwise they will simply be a parasitic attachment to it. It is difficult to see how Islam can contribute to this civilization while rejecting or questioning its premises." Allawi has it partly right and partly wrong. The roots of Western civilization are indisputably Christian. It is the task of historians of science and technology to explain why modern science arose in Christendom and not in the lands of Islam, where seemingly the groundwork had previously been laid. Modern science is the product of Western civilization and no other. The Enlightenment repudiation of the Hellenic and Christian sources of Western culture has in our own day borne its inexorable fruit in the crass materialism that is as offensive to Christians as it is to Muslims. Absent Christianity, the West has little to defend but its material culture. But that said, the historical difference between Christianity and Islam cannot be ignored. Allawi rightly identifies with the spirituality of the Prophet at Mecca, as can many non-Muslims, but he fails to come to grips with the Warrior Prophet of Medina who inspired the violent spread of Islam. The contradiction defies resolution.

Part II – Science and the Intelligibility of Nature

Gaukroger, Stephen. *The Emergence of a Scientific Culture; Science and the Shaping of Modernity 1210–1685.* Oxford: Clarendon Press, 2006. pp. ix + 563.

As the author tells us in his Introduction, he has set out to write a conceptual and cultural history of the emergence of a scientific culture in the West from the early modern period to the present. Gaukroger's study shows clearly that modern science is the outcome of a distinctive culture long in the making, a culture whose history begins in classical antiquity.

Scholars agree that since classical antiquity there have been a number of civilizations that have witnessed a scientific revolution. Gaukroger speaks of the "rich productive scientific cultures in which fundamental and especially intractable, physical, medical, astronomical, and other problems are opened up and dealt with in an innovative and concerted fashion, producing cumulative results over several generations." He identifies these as Greece and the Hellenic diaspora, Arab/Islamic North Africa/Near East/ Iberian Peninsula in the ninth, tenth, and eleventh centuries, Paris and Oxford in the thirteenth and fourteenth centuries, and China from the twelfth to the fourteenth centuries.

The "scientific revolution" of seventeenth- and eighteenth-century Europe is something different. Gaukroger's book is an attempt to answer the question: why did it occur in the West and in the modern era and why not in Greek antiquity, China, or medieval Paris and Oxford? The uninterrupted and cumulative growth of the scientific revolution of the early modern period, Gaukroger tells us, breaks with the boom/bust pattern of other cultures. Not only that, but the scientific revolution was so spectacular that it not only displaced competing accounts, but was extrapolated to all cognitive domains. In a relatively short time, Copernicanism and Darwinism came to replace firmly held philosophical and theological views concerning nature and order in nature that had persisted since biblical times.

Of the several themes that pervade this volume, the overarching theme is the fortune of Aristotelian natural philosophy from antiquity to the second half of the seventeenth century. By natural philosophy is understood something broader than a philosophy of nature. In the Aristotelian sense, natural philosophy is a unified, systematic way of understanding all natural phenomena, including the disciplines that we have come to recognize as physics, chemistry and biology. "For Aristotle," Gaukroger writes, "the identity of natural philosophy lay in its search for the intrinsic principles underlying natural phenomena, and this conception excludes a number of cognitive disciplines—practical mathematics, medicine, and natural history—on grounds that these are either not concerned with natural phenomena or do not pursue their inquiry in terms of underlying principles."

The dates of the subtitle need explaining. 1210 is the date of the first Paris condemnation of Aristotle. In that year the University of Paris banned all public and private teaching of Aristotle's philosophy in the Arts Faculty. 1685 marks the twilight, if not the demise, of Aristotelian natural philosophy and the ascendancy of a period dominated by the works of Locke, Newton, and Leibniz. From the thirteenth to the sixteenth century two models had provided for the unity of knowledge; one was the Aristotelian notion of *scientia,* the other, the Christian idea of a universe designed and created *ex nihilo* by a single God as an abode for human beings. In the seventeenth century both were confronted by nominalistic and mechanistic interpretations of nature and causality.

The scientific revolution advanced hypotheses and explanations that challenged both Aristotle's natural philosophy and Christian interpretations of nature. Darwin was thought to displace *Genesis,* Copernicus, a man-centered universe, and mechanism, the recognition of design in nature. Pagan philosophers had made natural philosophy the basis of moral philosophy. Aristotelian metaphysics had been employed by the early Church Fathers as they interpreted the texts of the Gospel. Justin Martyr, Marius Victorinus, and Clement of Alexandria recognized that Aristotelian natural philosophy, while not intrinsically Christian was nevertheless not inherently pagan. Although Aristotelian natural philosophy was not without rivals, notably those of the atomists and the neo-Platonic and Augustinian schools, it was to hold sway until the sixteenth century when it gave way to mechanistic interpretations of nature advanced by Gassendi, Mersenne, and Descartes.

Gassendi's natural philosophy was perhaps the most influcntial. Presented as a systematic matter-theory inspired by the Greek atomists, when combined with the doctrine of primary and secondary qualities, it did away with the concept of nature and with it teleology. Gassendi's mechanism, not to be confused with mechanics, offered a general picture of how the world is to be explained, what constitutes nature at its most basic level, and what kind of processes occur in it at that fundamental level. In its pre-Newtonian version, it is committed to explaining macroscopic phenomena in terms of microscopic corpuscles. Gassendi's atomism raised a number of questions that remain in contemporary philosophy of science. If there is no inner nature or essence of things, what is it that we grasp in cognition? What, indeed, is truth? Gaukroger promises to continue the narrative in a subsequent volume.

A short review cannot do justice to this volume or to Gaukroger's encyclopedic command of Western philosophy. In a final, thought-provoking chapter, rcminiscent of Etienne Gilson's *Unity of Philosophical Experience,* Gaukroger speaks to the unity of scientific knowledge. That chapter alone is worth thc price of this insightful book.

Guicciardini, Niccolò. *Isaac Newton on Mathematical Certainty and Method.* Cambridge Mass. The MIT Press, 2009. xxiii + 422 pp. Cloth, $55.00.

Newton's *Philosophiae Naturalis Principia Mathematica* (1687) has been called one of the most important single works in the history of modern science. Add to that his *Opticks* (1704), his discovery of infinitesimal calculus and the binomial theorem, his formulation of the three fundamental laws of motion, his analysis of white light, and one has yet only a partial image of his genius. Guicciardini's present work is an attempt to flesh out another aspect of Newton's thought, namely, his philosophy of mathematics. Guicciardini's study is not an attempt to comment on or to challenge D. T. Whiteside's eight-volume *Mathematical Papers* (1967–81) but is primarily an attempt to determine Newton's understanding of the role of mathematics in natural philosophy. With Descartes and Leibniz he aimed to introduce certainty into natural philosophy even if it meant parting company with his beloved Plato and Aristotle.

We speak of modern physics up to the coming of quantum mechanics as Newtonian physics. With Newton we have entered the age of Galileo, Kepler, Boyle, Halley, Descartes, Gassendi, and Leibniz, intellectual giants all. Seventeenth-century physics was replacing qualitative analysis of the ancients with quantitative precision. Newton clearly wrestled with the problem of how to relate the common and new algebraic analyses of the moderns with the venerated methods of the ancients. For him, large questions loomed. When is a geometrical construct exact? What guarantees the applicability of geometry to mechanics? In this context, Newton's mathematical work can be understood as a protracted development and response to Descartes. In a long-standing polemic against Descartes he resisted a purely mechanistic interpretation of natural phenomena. Guicciardini writes, "He sought certainty in mathematics, and never ceased to see mathematics as the vehicle for delivering certainty in natural philosophy. Opposed to the anti-classical stance that he perceived in Descartes' *Géométrie*, he portrayed himself as indebted to Euclid and Apollonius, rather than to the moderns."

To be kept in mind is Newton's distinction between analytic and synthetic method. For him, analysis consists in making experiments and observations and in deriving general conclusions from them by induction. Synthesis consists in assuming established laws, principles, or causes and explaining phenomena by deducing consequences from these laws. Mathematics is the mind's tool or instrument in the whole process. The motions to be studied must be measured and reduced to mathematical formula. Newton clearly sought the purification of physical science from classical metaphysics with its preoccupation with cause, whether ultimate or efficient causes, or what the Scholastics called formal causes. And yet he maintained that while the use of mathematics is necessary, it is not by itself a guarantee of scientific knowledge of the world. It is easy to find contemporary philosophers who would concur.

It should be noted that Niccolò Guicciardini is Professor of the History of Science at the University of Bergamo, Italy. He is the author of *The Development of Newtonian Calculus in Britain, 1700–1800* and *Reading the* Principia: *The Debate on Newton's Mathematical Methods for Natural Philosophy from 1687 to 1736*. This work only adds to his formidable stature as a scholar of the Newtonian period.

LoLordo, Antonia. *Pierre Gassendi and the Birth of Early Modern Philosophy.* Cambridge: Cambridge University Press, 2006. pp. x + 283.

This work is aptly subtitled "The Birth of Modern Philosophy." Pierre Gassendi (1592–1655) is not a household name, but he was in his own day engaged in one way or another with the leading intellectual figures of his time. He corresponded with scores of his illustrious contemporaries, notably with Descartes, Galileo, Kepler, Hobbes, Campanella, and Christina of Sweden. His influence on Locke has been noted; Mersenne was a close friend.

Although Gassendi was trained as a theologian in the Scholastic tradition, he chose to work as a philosopher. LoLordo's chapter headings alone indicate the breadth of his interests: "Gassendi's Philosophical Opponents," "Skepticism, Perception, and the Truth of Appearances," "Cognition, Knowledge and the Theory of Signs," "Space and Time," "Atoms and Causes," "Bodies and Motion," "Generation, Life, and the Corporeal Soul," and finally "Faith, Reason, and the Immaterial Soul."

Gassendi clearly stands at the threshold of modernity, anticipating the British empiricists by more than a century. It is Descartes and his artificially created "mind-body problem" that stimulated Gassendi to address the age-old problem of universals and the relation between sense and intellectual knowledge. In his criticism of Descartes, he writes, "When you say that you are simply a thing that thinks, you mention an operation that everyone was already aware of—but you say nothing about the substance carrying out this operation: what sort of substance is it, what it consists in, how it organizes itself in order to carry out its different functions . . . ." In LoLordo's judgment, "Were one a seventeenth century intellectual who finds Cartesianism unacceptable, Gassendi's philosophy was an obvious alternative."

LoLordo takes the reader through the evolution of Gassendi's thought from the *Exercitationes paradoxiae adversus Aristoteleos* (1624), the *Disquisitio Metaphysica* (1644), a critique of Descartes, and the posthumously published *Philosophiae Epicuri Syntagma* (1649). In doing so she documents the progression of Gassendi's thought, from his early skepticism to his eventual espousal of a mechanistic interpretation of nature. Confronted with startling advances in the natural sciences, the young Gassendi can no longer remain a skeptic. He is forced to develop a philosophical understanding of nature. Gassendi's resultant atomism is worthy of a study in itself. Many of the conceptual problems confronting the physics and chemistry of the seventeenth century remain in an analogous form today. One of Gassendi's dictums could well be inscribed as a classroom motto: "It is not permitted to transfer into Physics something abstractly demonstrated in Geometry."

The reader may find interesting the chronology of Gassendi's philosophical journey. We find him deeply engaged in criticism of the three main intellectual systems of his day, i.e., Scholastic Aristotelianism, Renaissance neo-Platonism, and the philosophy of Descartes, before he attempts to develop his own philosophical outlook. Many of his criticisms remain telling. Eventually Gassendi had to reconcile his mechanistic atomism with certain tenets of his Catholic faith, notably his belief in the immortality of the human soul, free will, and an infinite God. Having failed to grasp the fact that much of what he accepted on faith could be defended with the metaphysics of Aristotle, he seized upon the natural philosophy of Epicurus to ground both a theory of knowledge and the moral philosophy he was antecedently committed to hold.

A short review cannot do LoLordo's scholarship justice. This is more than a book about Gassendi. The author, by placing Gassendi within the context of the intellectual climate of his day, provides a valuable sketch of an entire period in the history of thought.

Blackwell, Richard J., *Behind the Scenes at Galileo's Trial.* Notre Dame, Ind., University of Notre Dame Press, 2006. pp. xiii + 245.

Without doubt "l'affaire Galileo," as Descartes called it, is one of the most studied events in the history of Western culture. The past four centuries have produced vast amounts of commentaries as well as countless interpretations and evaluations by physicists, astronomers, theologians, philosophers, churchmen, historians, and even playwrights. Almost sixty books were written about the trial from 1633-1651 alone, and one has yet to learn how many have been published since. Given the vast amount of literature produced just within the past fifty years, Richard Blackwell is almost apologetic for bringing out yet another volume. He is the author of numerous books and articles, including *Galileo, Bellarmine and the Bible* (1991), and is the translator of *A Defense of Galileo: the Mathematician from Florence* (1994). This adds to his already impressive stature as a chronicler of the famous event.

   Behind the Scenes is divided into two parts. The first part provides an informative overview of the elements that led to the trial of 1632. The second part consists of three appendices, i.e., Blackwell's translations of three behind-the-scenes documents that shed some light on the episode. It is difficult to say precisely when l'affaire Galileo actually began. Copernicus promulgated his heliocentric view of the universe as early as 1510 although publication of his complete work, *On the Revolution of the Celestial Spheres*, had to await 1543, the year of his death. For the greater part of a century ecclesiastical authorities made no official condemnation of a doctrine that seemingly contradicted Sacred Scripture. From Patristic times it was acknowledged that Sacred Scripture had to be interpreted at several levels, the literal meaning being only one. In fact, Antonio Foscarini, a Carmelite priest, in 1615 argued that the Copernican doctrine is both in agreement with the truth and not contrary to Sacred Scripture. Yet in 1616, shortly before Galileo published his *Dialogue Concerning the Two Chief World Systems*, the Copernican teaching was condemned. It is to be remembered that the heliocentric theory not only challenged a literal interpretation of the Bible but also the Ptolemaic/Aristotelian conception of the universe that supported the traditional Biblical interpretation. On February 26, 1616, in the presence of Cardinal Bellarmine, Galileo was served an injunction issued by the Holy Office demanding that he abandon his defense of Copernicanism, "nor henceforth to hold, teach or defend in any way, either verbally or in writing" the heliocentric view of the universe. Given Aristotelian standards regarding the nature of demonstration, Galileo could not prove that the earth revolved around the sun. Bellarmine clearly understood the difference between a hypothetical explanation and a demonstration and evidently had no trouble with Galileo's defense of the heliocentric view as an hypothesis. Apparently a *modus vivendi* was worked out to that effect. In fact, proof awaited the first part of the nineteenth century when astronomers for the first time were able to measure the parallax of the stars. Galileo was aware of the proscription and in an effort to garner support for his theory without directly promulgating a prohibited view produced his *Dialogue*. The discussion takes place among three parties, with Salviati defending the heliocentric view, Simplicio the Ptolemaic view and Sagredo open-mindedly commenting on each point made by Salviati. The literary device was a transparent defense of Galileo's own view and was seen as a violation of the injunction prohibiting the espousal of the Copernican view.

In the years after his trial and condemnation, Galileo remained convinced that his downfall had been caused by a plot against him by his enemies. Evidence of a plot may be lacking, but he certainly had enemies. His sharpest opponent was Christoph Scheiner, an astronomer, who fell out with Galileo twenty years before his trial over the issues of priority of observation and interpretation in regard to sun spots. Scheiner wrote personal attacks before and during the trial. Blackwell provides a translation of Scheiner's "Prodomus pro sole mobile" as an appendix to the present volume. Galileo's foremost critic was Melchior Inchofer, S.J., a theologian with no background in astronomy or

science, who was in a position to do him harm as advisor to the Holy
Office. Blackwell devotes forty percent of the volume to Inchofer's *A
Summary Treatise Concerning the Motion or Rest of the Earth and the
Sun, in which it is briefly shown what is and what is not to be held as
certain according to the teachings of Sacred Scriptures and the Holy
Fathers*. If the evidence does not support a plot in Galileo's sense,
Blackwell's account provides a scenario for a spellbinding novel.
English-speaking readers can be grateful for the author's translation of
Inchofer's behind-the-scenes document. The story leaves enough lati-
tude for the reader to draw his own conclusions. Although scholars both
acquit and condemn the Church, the underlying issue remains: what
constitutes a demonstration?

Meulders, Michel. *Helmholtz: From Enlightenment to Neuroscicnce.* Translated and edited by Laurence Garvey. Cambridge, Mass MIT Press, 2010. pp. xvii + 235.

Hermann von Helmholtz (1821–1894) is remembered as one of the leading figures of German physiology in the nineteenth century, especially for his work on the perception of color, for his contribution to neurophysiology, and for his invention of the ophthalmoscope.

An empiricist to the core, he was convinced that physiology played an indispensable role in an understanding of major psychological functions such as vision and the perception of color and space. He was opposed to the idealists and *naturphilosophen* who interpreted those functions from a viewpoint based on presuppositions that were inaccessible to experimentation. He argued vigorously against any attempt to explain nature by recourse to metaphysics. In discussions of the phenomenon of color, he found it ncccssary to oppose some of the scientific research of Johann Wolfgang von Goethe (1749–1832), who had written an influential book entitled, *Theory of Colours.* Goethe resisted any purely mechanistic interpretation of psychological phenomena.

The book, it should be noted, is not merely about Helmholtz. Michel Meulders, former Dean of the Medical School and Professor Emeritus of Neuroscience of the Catholic University of Louvain, provides an interesting sketch of the scientific atmosphere and cultural milieu of the early nineteenth century. An entire chapter is devoted to a discussion of the natural philosophy of the day, an outlook he shows to be the indispensable background for an understanding of science and medicine in Germany in the early part of that century.

In subsequent chapters, Meulders summarizes and analyzes Helmholtz's principal scientific achievements. Two works of major importance are singled out for analysis—namely, *The Handbook of Physiological Optics, Vision and Perception,* and *Sensation of Tone as a Physiological Basis for the Theory of Music.* A significant part of

Helmholtz: From Enlightenment to Neuroscience is devoted to a discussion of the scientific work of Goethe, given Helmholtz's opposition to much of Goethe's work on color and Goethe's rejection of Enlightenment philosophy in general. Goethe is quoted as saying, "If you show a red flag to a bull, it becomes angry, but a philosopher begins to rage as soon as you merely speak of color."

Helmholtz, in spite of his acknowledged achievements, was not himself immune to criticism from renowned contemporaries such as Wilhelm Wundt, a former student, Ernst Mach, and William James. Interesting, too, he was not viewed in a good light by Lenin who accused him of Kantianism, subjectivism, and agnosticism. In mid-life Helmholtz abandoned his work in the life sciences to concentrate in physics, notably in areas such as electricity and thermodynamics. Always faithful to Kant, Helmholtz held that intuition meant seizing in a single act the raw results of sensory representation but in the context of the a priori forms of space and time. Fortified by this certainty of obtaining knowledge safely, the scientist could, through observation and inductive research, investigate the laws of nature. Those laws when expressed in words would be considered mere hypotheses in need of verification by further certification with facts. It is only by proceeding with careful observation that one can assume them to be correct and legitimate, at least under given experimental conditions. For Helmholtz the scientist is something like a prophet or magician insofar as he has acquired power over nature and is able to predict the occurrence of certain phenomena.

This is an insightful book, not exactly bedside reading, but a book that will give the novice an insight into the conceptual opposition between the inherited natural philosophy of the nineteenth century and the empiricism of Locke and Hume, which seemed to account better for the remarkable achievements of what we know as modern science.

Nye, Mary Jo. *Michael Polanyi and His Generation: Origins of the Social Construction of Science.* Chicago: University of Chicago Press, 2011. pp. xxi + 405.

This is a chronicle of the scientific achievements of Michael Polanyi, but it is more than that. It is a description of the scientific, political, and cultural landscape of Europe from World War I to the Cold War. Nye follows Polanyi's life and career from his birth (1891) in Budapest to his death in Manchester at the age of 84 (1976). She documents Polanyi's many scientific achievements, but the strength of the volume is her description of the scientific communities in which he flourished, first in Budapest, then in Weimar Berlin, and finally in Manchester. Polanyi earned a medical degree in 1913 and a Ph.D. in physical chemistry in 1917 at the University of Budapest. With the dissolution of the Austro-Hungarian Empire following the Great War, many Hungarian scientists trained in Budapest found it expedient to leave Hungary. Eugene Wigner, John von Neumann, Leo Szilard, and Edward Teller were among the Hungarian émigrés. Some found refuge in Germany, others in England. Polanyi chose to further his study of physical chemistry at Karlsruhe but in 1920 moved to Berlin to work at the Kaiser Wilhelm Institute for Fiber Chemistry. Berlin of the 1920s was the city of Einstein, Planck, Fritz Haber, Walter Nernst, and Lisa Meitner. Weimar Berlin had become the cultural center of Central and Eastern Europe. Besides the Humboldt University, suburban Dahlem was the site of seven scientific institutes.

The racial policies of the National Socialist Party eventually forced Polanyi to leave Germany. After first declining, Polanyi accepted a chair in chemistry at the University of Manchester in 1933. By 1940 his interests had shifted to economics and social and political philosophy, and he exchanged the chair in chemistry for one in social philosophy. In 1951 he was offered a chair in social philosophy at the University of Chicago, a position that he was unable to accept because he was denied a visa by the U.S. State Department, no doubt because his name was associated with the leftist politics of his brother Karl who had supported the Soviet economic policies of the 1920s and l930s.

Nye is especially interested in the social nature of science, in the close-knit families of physicists and chemist who comprised the scientific communities of Budapest and Berlin. Polanyi's views on the nature of science are worthy of a treatise unto itself. Science, he held, is a community of dogmatic traditions and social practices, not a march of revolutionary or skeptical ideas. Polanyi describes his own scientific investigations as ordinary, typical of science, "natural science," in Thomas Kuhn's use of the term. "The popular notion of a straightforward relationship between empirical data and scientific discovery or verification is rooted in a misunderstanding of how science really works." Good evidence is often ignored when a community of opinion favors one opinion over another. He describes as pernicious the simple prescription of nineteenth-century positivism and logical empiricism as naïve. Bertrand Russell is a target, for Russell had written, "The triumphs of science are due to the substitution of observation and inference for authority in intellectual matters. Every attempt to revive authority in intellectual matters is a retrograde step." "Nothing could be further from the truth," argues Polanyi, citing his own experience, his career, and authority structures in science.

The scientific community of Weimar Berlin was in a sense detached from the social and political turmoil that was destroying the Republic. In describing the situation, James Crowther, a reporter for the *Manchester Guardian* upon visiting Berlin in 1930, wrote: " I was left with the impression the brilliant scientific effervescence . . . had an intellectual life of its own, above that of industry and the people, in spite of the integration of the scientific research with industry. This division of high intellectual life from the rumblings underneath was one of the most striking features of the Weimar Republic." Polanyi's mother had a different perspective: "The times in Berlin are beginning to be frightful," she wrote to a friend in Budapest, "unemployment, privation, and disheveled economic, political and emotional life. One says the worst will come in January, the other in February . . . but that it will come, they all believe." (67)

Nye devotes an entire chapter to the reception of Polanyi's *Personal Knowledge,* a book based on his Gifford Lectures of 1951–52. Of the book, Nye writes, "Polanyi's realism appealed to many scientists who found his account of scientific life and scientists' behavior more recognizable than most philosophers' or historians' analyses. The religious tone of the realism was also congenial to many scientists. The spiritual dimension of *Personal Knowledge* found favor among Christians, and his discussion of cosmic evolution proved useful to proponents of teleology and intelligent design in arguments against mainstream evolutionary biology."

With respect to economic theory, Polanyi took the side of von Hayek and von Mises. The economy, he maintained, is not to be used for social engineering. Economic theory based on political preferences is no substitute for natural laws. He agreed with von Hayek that if a depression seems underway, any attempt to cure it by monetary and fiscal policy will likely worsen the situation. A slump in a trade cycle is a sign that the system will head back to equilibrium and should be left alone. Patience must reign during inevitable periods of unemployment, and an elastic supply of currency makes the situation worse—not better.

No brief review can do justice to this densely packed book. Those interested in Polanyi's insider account of the nature of scientific investigation can be grateful for Mary Jo Nye's painstaking research.

Manicas, Peter T. *A Realist Philosophy of Science: Explanation and Understanding.* Cambridge: Cambridge University Press, 2006. pp. ix + 225.

Writing from a realist perspective, Manicas addresses the problem of explanation in the social sciences. He defends the thesis that the fundamental goal of both natural and social sciences is not prediction and control, or even the explanation of events, but rather the understanding of the processes that jointly produce the contingent outcomes of experience. Scientific knowledge, he maintains, consists primarily in a knowledge of the internal structures of persisting things and materials and secondarily in a knowledge of the statistics of events, or of the behavior of such things and materials. Scientific understanding occurs when causal analysis enables us to explain how the patterns discerned amidst the flux of events are produced by the persisting natures and constitutions of things.

Chapter one is a compelling critique of David Hume and the positivist view that reduces science to description and prediction. If the goal of science is to understand the processes of nature, we must identify the causal mechanisms that are at work in the world. Once these are understood, all sorts of phenomena are rendered intelligible. Manicas makes a distinction between "scientific explanation" and "understanding." The two are not the same although we sometimes use the words interchangeably. Understanding is achieved when explanation includes a well-confirmed theory about the generative mechanism responsible for the phenomena under investigation. Phenomena that are unintelligible in terms of themselves beg to be explained causally. A successful theoretical explanation consists of a representation of the structure of the enduring system in which the events under consideration occur. This is accomplished when the mechanism responsible for its generation is identified

Manicas draws heavily on Rom Harré's *Principles of Scientific Thinking* (1970), a work in which Harré develops an account of explanation in the natural sciences, which Manicas analogously employs as he describes what he calls the "ontological status" of the social sciences. Understanding in the social sciences, Manicas argues, is achieved when, as in the physical sciences, we can exhibit a causal mechanism responsible for the phenomenon in question. He does not deny that there are important differences between the scientific study of nature and the scientific study of society. "In our world, most events—birth, growth, rain, fires, earthquakes, depressions, revolutions—are products of a complex nexus of causes of many kinds that are conjunctively at work." It is for this reason that "the natural sciences, instead of seeking to explain concrete events, more modestly, seek to understand the mechanisms and processes of nature." He offers as an example, "We understand why planets move in ellipses, why materials burn, why salt dissolves in water (when it does) when we have a physical theory that provides a causal mechanism." This understanding is accomplished by providing principles detailing the structure of molecules, the atomic structure of salt and water, principles of their action, and so on. Thus equipped one can understand the causal mechanisms at work that explain oxidation and dissolution, that is, combustion and solubility. Causal mechanisms are often inferred. No one has seen a photon, but photons are among the important nonobservable particles posited in physical theory that facilitate an understanding of a wide range of phenomena. Enrico Fermi, years before the actual discovery of the neutrino, successfully incorporated that inferred particle in his theory of beta decay.

Manicas will say that although everything is caused, there is a radical contingency in both natural and human history. As with the natural sciences, the task of the social sciences is to understand how social mechanisms *structure* but do not determine outcomes. Generative social mechanisms in the social sciences are always historically situated. In fact, the generative mechanisms of social processes are the actions of human persons. Social science seeks to explain concrete events and episodes, for example, the collapse of a regime, an economic depression, a dramatic rise in divorces, why working-class kids get working-class jobs, and why, when religious institutions are weakened, there is a loss of normative control. In these cases, explanation takes the form of a narrative that identifies the critical social mechanisms at work and links them sequentially to the contingent but causally pertinent acts of persons. Understanding presupposes good description, both quantitative and qualitative. History, of course, is a special case. In history there are neither laws nor sets of conditions from which one makes determinative calculations. To explain some actual outcomes, one needs to go back in time and identify sequentially the pertinent causes as they combine to produce outcomes. This requires a narrative that links critical actions and events with ongoing social processes grasped in terms of social mechanisms. Manicas reminds us that in history there are neither laws nor sets of conditions from which one can make deterministic calculations.

It is easy to be enthusiastic about *A Realist Philosophy of Science*. The book is not only a comprehensive treatment of "explanation" in the social sciences but has the merit of being well written, factual, and informative. Manicas is the voice of wisdom and sanity in a field where positivistic assumptions regarding the nature of science often go unchallenged.

Giere, Ronald N. *Scientific Perspectivism.* Chicago: University of Chicago Press, 2006. ix + 151 pp. Cloth, $30.00.

Ronald N. Giere is professor of philosophy emeritus at the University of Minnesota, a former director of the Minnesota Center for the Philosophy of Science, and a past president of the Philosophy of Science Association. The present work, he tells us, is the fruit of decades of reflection and builds upon his previously published volume, *Philosophy without Laws.* "The primary objective of *Scientific Perspectivism*," he writes, "is to develop an understanding of scientific claims that mediates between the strong objectivism of most scientists or the hard realism of most philosophers of science and the constructivism found largely among historians and sociologists of science." Giere is convinced that the so-called "constructivists" have a valid point. "Everyone," he concedes, "starts out a common sense realist," believing that things are what they are thought to be. But if one begins to examine scientific practice, objective realism becomes hard to defend. Giere is led eventually to the conclusion: "For a perspectival realist, the strongest claims a scientist can legitimately make are of a qualified, conditional form, i.e. 'according to this highly confirmed theory (or reliable instrument) the world seems such and such.'" Giere is content to leave it at that. "There is no way legitimately to take the further objectivist step and declare unconditionally, 'this theory (or instrument) provides us with a complete and literally correct picture of the world itself.'"

The main thrust of the arguments presented in this book is to show that the practice of science supports the perspectival rather than an objectivist understanding of scientific realism. Claims to knowledge, Giere is convinced, are determined in part by the research process. Scientists interpret results partly in terms of their own expertise, partly by reason of the available instrumentation, and partly on the basis of their judgment as to which approach provides the most opportunity for doing new work, whether experimental or theoretical.

Given that scientific claims may be in part socially constructed, to validate any claim, it is imperative that we uncover the social contribution that may lay unperccived. This can only be determined, if at all, by a detailed historical examination of the claim in question. Scientific enquiry is so infused with all sorts of human values and judgments that what ends up being proclaimed to be the structure of reality may have little resemblance to the structure of the real world. Investigators often see what is in their social interest to see. Furthermore, some degree of contingency is always present in science."

In defending his perspectival position, Giere provides an extensive review of the literature promoting the realist view and of the literature defending the constructivist view. He concedes points to both views, finally concluding that if scientific knowledge is regarded as perspectival, "scientific claims are neither as objective as objectivist realists think nor as socially determined as moderate constructivists claim." Perspectival realism, he claims, is as much realism as science can provide.

In support of his view, reflecting on the actual practice of science itself, Giere devotes chapters to a discussion of color vision, to the involvement of instrumentation in virtually all scientific observation, and to the use of physical and abstract models in scientific theorizing. His examples are well chosen and do in fact support his thesis. Giere's book could well be read as a preface to Stephen Gaukroger's *The Emergence of a Scientific Culture: Science and the Shaping of Modernity 1210–1685*. The latter reinforces Giere's perspectivism while maintaining a realist understanding of the nature of scientific enquiry.

Groarke, Louis. *An Aristotelian Account of Induction: Creating Something from Nothing.* McGill-Queens University Press, Montreal and Kingston, 2009. pp. xiv + 467. Cloth, $95.00; Paper, $32.95.

This work is best regarded as a defense of the first principles of thought and being from an Aristotelian point of view. Clearly it is a critique of the empiricist account of induction and of the empiricist notion of "substance." Defending Aristotle against the charge of naïve realism, early in the volume Groarke challenges Wittgenstein's claim that induction has no logical justification, only a psychological one. In a chapter, "Before and After Hume," his adversary is not only David Hume but John Locke and René Descartes as well.

In this space, given the density of the book, all that can be done is to call attention to its content. If you have forgotten your Venn diagrams or Hamiltonian notations, this will provide a refresher course and at the same time indicate their limitations or usefulness. There are chapters entitled, "A Deductive Account of Induction," "Five Levels of Induction," an interesting and valuable chapter on moral induction, and another on creativity. The final chapter, "Where Science Comes to an End," is worth the price of the book. This is an extensively researched work as its 20-page bibliography will attest. It is hard to believe that any contemporary who has written on the subject has escaped Groarke's notice or that one can imagine a more learned account of the *status quaestionis*.

Harper, William L. *Isaac Newton's Scientific Method: Turning Data into Evidence about Gravity and Cosmology.* Oxford: Oxford University Press, 2011. Pp.xvii + 424.

A classic example illustrative of the nature of the scientific method is found in Isaac Newton's *Mathematical Principles of Natural Philosophy* (1687), called one of the most important single works in the history of modern science. We speak of modern physics up to the age of quantum mechanics as Newtonian physics. With Newton we enter the age of Galileo, Kepler, Boyle, Halley, Gassendi, and Leibniz, intellectual giants all. In the seventeenth century physics turned from qualitative analysis to quantitative precision. As William Harper shows, Newton wrestled with the problem of how to relate common new algebraic analyses of modern approaches with the venerated methods of the ancients. For Newton, large questions begged to be answered. When is a geometrical construct exact? What guarantees the applicability of geometry to mechanics?

In his exposition of Newton's method, Harper traces the steps by which Newton argued from the phenomenon of orbital motion to centripetal forces and then to universal gravity. This in turn enabled him to calculate the masses of the sun and the planets from orbits about them, and further it led to the decisive resolution of the problem of deciding between the empirical equivalence of the heliocentric and geocentric world systems. Newton concluded that neither is completely accurate because both the sun and the earth are moving relative to the center of the solar system. The sun, he finds, never recedes very far from the center of this mass, thus making it possible to achieve proximate calculations of the complex motion of the planets by successively more accurate models. Newton employed the notion of gravity as a physical cause to explain planetary motion in general, even though he was unable to find the initial cause of orbital motion itself. Having established that all celestial bodies are kept in their orbits by the centripetal forces of gravity, Newton calculated those forces to be the inverse of the square of the distance from their centers.

As the familiar model of scientific investigation would have it, hypotheses are verified by conclusions drawn from them, or put another way, empirical success is determined by and limited to accurate predictions. Newton differs from what has become the positivist understanding of science. In addition to accurate prediction, he held, a theory must attempt to explain, to exhibit a cause for the phenomena in question. A true explanation turns theoretical questions into ones which can be empirically answered by the measurement of relevant phenomena, but more than that, theoretical propositions inferred from phenomena specify their parameters, and, when successful, function provisionally to serve as guides to further research.

Harper distances Newton from the basic hypothetic/deductive model for scientific method that dominated much discussion by philosophers of science in the twentieth century. "Newton's method," he writes, "differs by adding features that go beyond the basic H-D model. One important addition is the richer ideal of empirical success that is realized in Newton's classic inferences from phenomena. The richer ideal of empirical success requires not just accurate predictions of phenomena, it requires in addition accurate measurement of the parameters by the predicted phenomena." Harper subsequently defends Newton against some contemporary challenges to his basically Aristotelian realism.

A short review cannot do this profound work justice. In sequentially organized chapters Harper discusses from Book Three, Proposition 1 through 13 of Newton's *Mathematical Principles of Natural Philosophy*. In a section entitled, "Lessons from Newton's own Scientific Method," Harper spells out in detail the inductive insight that led Newton to formulate his laws of motion and their corollaries. The book ends with a postscript, "Measurement and evidence—Newton's method at work in cosmology today." Harper cites a work by Robert Kirshner, *The Extravagant Universe*, as evidence that Newton's method for turning data into evidence still guides cosmology today.

Fantoli, Annibale. *The Case of Galileo: A Closed Question?* Trans. George V. Coyne. Notre Dame, Indiana: University of Notre Dame Press. 2012. Pp. Xii + 271.

The facts are indisputable. Aristarchus of Samos (310–230 B.C.) proposed in ancient Greece a sun-centered system. Nicholas Copernicus (1473–1543) promulgated his heliocentric theory as early as 1510, although publication of his complete work, *On the Revolution of the Heavenly Spheres*, a mathematical defense of the heliocentric system, had to await 1543, the year of his death. Copernicus showed that all that was required to explain the phenomena in the heavens was to put the sun in the center instead of the earth, attribute motion to the earth, i.e., daily rotation on its axis and orbital motion around the sun. Copernicus calculated that the earth's axis to the plane of its elliptical motion to be 23.5 degrees. His theory had the merit of simplicity, but it seemed to contradict common sense and Sacred Scripture. In a preface to *On the Revolution of the Heavenly Spheres*, the Protestant editor, Andreas Osiander, wrote that Copernicus's theory should be considered a pure mathematical hypothesis and not a physical explanation of the heavens. Johannes Kepler was shortly to do away with the assumption of circular orbits assigned to the planets. Copernicus's book sold 500 copies within a short time but did not undergo a second edition until twenty-three years later.

Enter Galileo (1564–1642). With lenses provide by Kepler, Galileo constructed a crude telescope but adequate enough for Galileo to discover the satellites of the planet Jupiter. With that and other observations the Aristotelian principle of the incorruptibility of the heavens was shattered. Ptolemaic astronomy was soon to be replaced. Galileo's observations convinced him that Copernicus was right, and he published the results of his observations in his book, The Starry Messenger (1610). Tycho Brahe (1546–1601), the most famous of the period's astronomers, could not endorse the Copernican theory except as a hypothetical explanation because it lacked proof. Aristotle's cosmology may have been undermined, but his distinction between demonstrative proof and a hypothetical explanation remained then, as it does today. If one could only measure the parallax of the stars, the heliocentric claim would be settled. Aristarchus thought as much, so did Brahe, and even Galileo sought the proof that eluded him. The Copernican theory remained just that until Friedrich Bessel's successful measurement of stellar parallax in 1838. Beyond doubt, the earth was shown to move against the background of the remote heavens.

Twenty years after *Starry Messenger*, Galileo published *Dialogue Concerning the Two Chief World Systems* in which he hoped to eliminate, in the light of new astronomical findings, common-sense opposition to the Copernican view. The *Dialogue* was at once polemical and pedagogical. Galileo was aware that he could not produce a rigorously valid and decisive proof of the heliocentric view, but he nevertheless held that the preponderance of evidence favored the Copernican system. The book drew renewed attention to Galileo's claims and renewed opposition in spite of the fact that the *Dialogue* ended somewhat ambiguously, with Galileo accused by some of playing to both sides of the debate. The story becomes ever more complicated at this point.

In the "Prologue" to *The Case of Galileo* Fantoli opens his book dramatically with Galileo on February 26, 1616, on his knees, in the presence of Cardinal Bellarmine, swearing that "after having been judicially instructed with injunction by the Holy Office to abandon completely the false opinion that the sun is the center of the world and does not move and the earth is not the center of the world and moves and not to hold, defend or teach these false doctrines in any way whatever, orally or in writing, and after having been notified that this doctrine is contrary to Holy Scripture, I wrote and published a book in which I treat this already condemned doctrine and adduce very effective reasons in its favor. . . . I abjure, curse and detest the above mentioned heresies." With the publication of *Dialogue Concerning the Two Chief World Systems* Galileo seemed to be going back on his sworn word and he was brought to trial again in 1633.

How did it come to this? Galileo had not been able to demonstrate the truth of the Copernican system, and, if he had followed the advice of friends and taught the system *ex supposito* as a hypothetical explanation, the trial may not have occurred. On the other hand, if the theologians had not needlessly insisted on a literal interpretation of the Hebrew Scriptures, the matter may not have come to a head. Serious scholars differ on the assessment of blame. Galileo had both friends and enemies. He could cite some support from the Collegio Romano, but the Dominicans remained hostile, not only because they were defending an inherited Ptolemaic/Aristotelian worldview, but in the opinion of one commentator because of some offense or slight on Galileo's part. For a description the personalities and warring factions involved, Fantoli may well be read in consort with Richard Blackwell's *Behind the Scenes at Galileo's Trial* and Maurice Finocchiaro's *Retrying Galileo*.

In the years after his second trial and condemnation Galileo remained convinced that his downfall had been caused by a plot against him by his enemies. Evidence of a plot may be lacking, but he did have enemies. His sharpest opponent was Christopher Scheiner, an astronomer, who fell out with Galileo twenty years before the second trial over the issues of priority of observations and interpretations with regard to sun spots. Another critic was Melchior Inchofer, S.J., a theologian with no background in astronomy or science, who was in a position to harm him as advisor to the Holy Office.

Without doubt the *l'affaire Galileo*, as Descartes was to call it, is one of the most studied events in the history of Western culture. By Finocchiaro's account, almost sixty books were written about the trial during the period 1633–1651. Add to that the vast numbers of commentaries, countless interpretations and evaluations that have been advanced by physicists, astronomers, theologians, philosophers, churchmen, historians, and even playwrights over the last four centuries. The trial was seized upon by D'Alembert, Voltaire, and other Enlightenment figures to bash the Church. Domenico Bernini, for one, contributed to the invention and diffusion of myths about the affair when he maliciously asserted that Galileo was held in an Inquisition prison for five years. Voltaire picked up the theme and either in ignorance or hatred wrote that Galileo was thrown into prison and made to fast on bread and water. Of course, Galileo was never imprisoned in any usual sense. When in Rome, his "prison" was the Palace of the Duke of

Tuscany, where he was treated as an honored guest; so too when he endured confinement as the guest of the Archbishop of Siena. As to his house arrest, one might envy Galileo, who in his late sixties was obliged to live out his last years in his country home at Arceti overlooking a beautiful valley outside of Firenze.

In November 1979 at a celebration to commemorate the centennial of Albert Einstein's birth, Pope John Paul II called for a reopening of the Galileo Affair. A Vatican commission was subsequently appointed with a view to the rehabilitation of Galileo. Paul Cardinal Poupard, thirteen years later in 1992, made the formal report of the commission at a meeting of the Pontifical Academy of the Sciences, with John Paul II in attendance. In his own speech after receiving the report, John Paul II seemed to be admitting not only that Church authorities had been in error but had acted unjustly, something Descartes in his day would not have conceded. As subsequently reported the condemnation of Galileo was itself seemingly condemned. Whatever its intent, John Paul II's speech has not ended the centuries-old controversy. Galileo's rehabilitation has merely started a new episode of Galileo studies. Bellarmine has his defenders even in the secular academy.

One must acknowledge that George Coyne has beautifully rendered into English Annibale Fantoli's original Italian text.

Feiner, Shmuel and Natalie Naimark-Goldberg. *Cultural Revolution in Berlin: Jews in the Age of Enlightenment.* Oxford, Bodleian Library, 2011. pp. ix + 94.

The focus of this brief historical study is the absorption by Jewish intellectuals of the prevailing civil and rational values of eighteenth-century Europe. It is a study of emancipation and Jewish integration into the wider society without loss of Jewish identity. The story here presented is entirely based on one collection of texts held in the Leopold Muller Memorial Library of the Oxford Center for Hebrew and Jewish studies. As such, the volume is richly illustrated by photographs of the books and manuscripts mentioned in the book that are held by the library.

Moses Mendelssohn (1729–1786), the central figure in this narrative, is representative of a new Jewish elite, which having adopted the basic values of the European Enlightenment, challenged the cultural supremacy of the rabbinical elite. Mendelssohn, who became fluent in German and other European languages, is acclaimed for prodding his fellow Jews to leave the ghetto, learn the German language, and embrace modernity, while at the same time counseling them to retain their religious tradition. His interest in natural theology led him to the study of Leibniz, Wolff, and Locke, among others. His treatise *Phaedo: On the Immortality of the Soul* (1767) underwent eleven editions in his lifetime. His greatest contribution to the Jewish Enlightenment is thought to be his book, *The Paths to Peace.* In it, he stressed the importance of making the Bible the chief object of study rather than the study of the Talmud, which is usually considered the authoritative text of the Jewish religious tradition. He translated the Bible into high German.

There followed a great secular revolution within the culture of the Jewish community. German had rarely been used by Jews in their daily lives. Hebrew hardly lent itself to the translation of scientific texts. Leaders of the secular movement were greatly disturbed by the neglect of the sciences. Meir Neumark assumed the role of translating many scientific texts for a Jewish audience who did not know Latin. Others were concerned that the neglect of grammar by rabbis and other commentators had led to a deplorable misinterpretation of the Scriptures and to a shameful misreading of other literature. The *Guide for the Perplexed* by the famous medieval philosopher and theologian, Moses Maimonides, was republished in 1742, having been out of print for nearly two hundred years.

Raphael Levi's pursuit of science brought the observant Jew into contact with non-Jewish knowledge and non-Jewish intellectuals, providing a model for others. Hartwig Wessely, for his part, outlined in 1782 the first systematic curriculum for modern Jewish education. Wessely employed a distinction between two modes of knowledge, "the teaching of man" or human knowledge and the "teaching of God" or divine knowledge. The study of the Bible and the Talmud, he maintained, should leave room for the study of history, geography, and natural science for these disciplines are necessary for a study of the ancient texts. He considered important the study of the vernacular from an early age. Wessely, although clearly a man of the eighteenth-century Enlightenment, a man comfortable in European culture, nevertheless did not lose his commitment to faith, to the study of the Bible and the Talmud and to the observance of the commandments, but on the other hand he no longer belonged to the circle of Talmudic scholars.

By the end of the eighteenth century there had emerged a formidable group of "free thinkers," a Jewish elite, who, in the light of their affinity for the values and concepts of the European Enlightenment, were prone to distinguish themselves from the Jewish masses. A typical representative of the reformed Jew was Lazarus Bendavid (1762-1832), a disciple of Immanuel Kant whose writing he helped to popularize. Bendavid blamed the Jews themselves for their negative image and insularity. In a Kantian manner, he sought to retain the Jewish religion in its "inner essence" while totally rejecting its rituals. Whereas Mendelssohn believed that the unique essence of Judaism lay in the obligation to observe the practical commandments, Bendavid put forth the radical idea of totally annulling the commandments as an essential step to ensure the acceptance of Jews in the modern world. Bendavid, we are told, was a prolific and dynamic intellectual, active in numerous enlightened German societies, and he even presided over some of them.

Bendavid was not alone. Saul Ascher (1767–1822) proposed a religious reform as a prerequisite for the acceptance of Jews as full citizens of the state. Following Kant, he also held that the law-based character of Judaism was opposed to the "true autonomy of the will" and irrelevant to the new generation. His criticism of rabbinic culture apart, it must be acknowledged that Ascher was among the few Jewish German intellectuals who dared engage in a direct confrontation with contemporary foes of the Jews, notably Johann Gottlieb Fichte, one of the founders of the Humboldt University of Berlin.

Feiner and Naimark-Goldberg end their narrative abruptly with the close of the eighteenth century. We know that within the German-speaking lands of nineteenth and early twentieth centuries, assimilated Jews not only flourished but became leaders in the sciences and in the arts. Budapest, Vienna, Munich, and Berlin became important centers for the study of theoretical physics and physical chemistry, and Jews are associated with major discoveries in each. Budapest alone gave birth to Eugene Wigner, John von Neumann, Leo Szilard, Michael Polanyi, and Edward Teller. Albert Einstein, born in Ulm, studied in Munich, Lise Meitner in Vienna. Moses Mendelssohn's grandson, Felix, earned world renown as a composer. Without doubt the cultural revolution produced great scientists who for the most part remained aloof to Enlightenment philosophy, often at variance with actual practice in the sciences.

Part III – Aids to the Understanding of Islam

Allawi, Ali A. *The Crisis of Islamic Civilization.* – New Haven: Yale University Press, 2009. pp. xvi + 304; $27.50 (Cloth).

While this is not a metaphysical treatise, it may be considered a philosophical attempt to understand the age-old faith vs. reason problem as bequeathed by medieval Islam, but it is more than that. The present book, Allawi tells his reader, is the product of "one person's attempt to understand the factors behind the spiritual decay of Islam and what the future holds if this process is not halted or reversed." The book focuses not on Islam from its founding, or on historical Islam, but on Islam of the last two hundred years, from the early nineteenth century when Western imperialism forced an encounter with modernity for which Islam was ill prepared. It should be noted be that Ali A. Allawi possesses not only extraordinary learning as a cultural historian but significant practical experience. He has served in the Iraqi postwar governments as Minister of Trade, Minister of Defense, and Minister of Finance. That learning and experience give this narrative an authoritative character which in other hands it might not possess.

Allawi approaches his topic with a description of the Iraq of his youth, the Iraq of the 1950s, a period in which the ruling class and the cultural and intellectual elites had moved far away from an overt identification with Islam. "Islam," he writes, "was not a noticeable factor in daily life. Religion was a mandatory course in school. . . (but) nobody taught us the rules of prayer or expected us to fast in Ramadan. . . . Women, not only in my own family but throughout the urban middle class, wore only Western clothes." The only connection with a pre-modern past, he relates, was that his grandfather always wore the "distinguishing and dignified dress of robes and turbans of an old-line merchant." Allawi continues, "I don't recall ever coming across the word 'jihad' in any contemporary context. The prevailing rhetoric had more to do with Arab destiny and anti-imperialism."

Secularism, he tells us, had the Muslim world by the throat. "Modernity was flooding in everywhere and people seemed to want more of it. Cinemas and snack bars, cabarets and country clubs, freely flowing alcohol and mixed parties, Baghdad was turning into Babylon, its hedonistic predecessor of yore. And it was not much different. . . in Casablanca, Cairo, Damascus, Istanbul, Tehran, Karachi and Jakarta."

But the cultural climate began to change in the 1960s and not simply because of ascendant military dictatorships throughout much of the Muslim world. Almost imperceptibly there had begun a re-spiritualization of Islam. The period called for reflection. The Muslim world was confronted with the fading of its own civilization, increasing indifference and outright abandonment of the foundational and spiritual bases of the faith. By the end of the 1970s, spiritual Islam as a way of worship became eclipsed by a resurgent militant, political, and violent Islam that increasingly seemed to define Islam in–the eyes of the West. In Allawi's judgment, "political Islam" is but a manifestation of an ailment rather than the ailment itself. Sectarian, ethnic, and racial hatreds continuously trump the ideals of Islamic unity. "The murderous violence unleashed by Wahhabi-inspired Islamists was accompanied by laborious jurisprudential 'justifications.' These were accepted by a large number of Muslims worldwide, and they legitimized the indiscriminate slaughter of innocent civilians."

While Muslims may have a common political culture and may share other affinities, there is no real political unity among them. The idea of a pan-Islamic unity as a realistic goal of political action is as chimerical as a union, let's say, of the English-speaking world.–In spite of ideological unity at one level, the natural state of Islam is diversity— a broad range of sects and groups exist within it. Yet, in Allawi's judgment, given the three power blocs confronting Islam—namely, the United States, a mercantilist China and an expanding European Union—Muslim countries may have to forge a power bloc unique to themselves in the financial arena to bypass the Bretton Woods institutions such as the World Bank and the International Monetary Fund. The latter, he thinks, along with the World Trade Organization are largely subservient to the interests of Western powers.

In explaining the title of the book, Allawi writes, "The crisis of Islamic civilization arises from the fact that it has been thwarted from demarcating its own pathways into contemporary life. The Western world of modernity has been superimposed on its own world view, and Islam has been unable to relate to the modern world except through this awkward and painfully alien framework." Contemporary Islam, obviously overwhelmed by the West, now faces globally imposed impersonal technological and market forces.–To the contrary, "The ethics of spiritualized Islam are based on a foundation of courtesy and modesty; courtesy toward the names and attributes of God, modesty in terms of the individual's affirmation of these traits as God's alone. . . Some of God's attributes cannot be reproduced in human form—for instance, His oneness or His everlastingness. Others are, such as mercy, compassion, gentleness and beauty."

Allawi rejects Samuel P. Huntington's thesis in *A Clash of Cultures* wherein Huntington speaks of a confrontation between Islam and Christianity. The "clash" as Allawi sees it is between the secular materialist culture of the West and the spiritual culture of Islam, with its emphasis on the worship of a transcendent God. "If Muslims want the very things that modern technological civilization promises . . . they will have to acknowledge the roots of that civilization in order to become an active and creative part of it. Otherwise they will simply be a parasitic attachment to it. It is difficult to see how Islam can contribute to this civilization while rejecting or questioning its premises." Participation in the dominant civilizational order entails, he believes, the risk of fatally undermining whatever is left of the Muslim's basic identity and autonomy. Allawi ends the book, given his perspective, on a somewhat pessimistic note, "If Muslims do not muster the inner resources of their faith to fashion a civilizing outer presence, then Islam as a civilization may indeed disappear."

Lacroix, Stéphane. *Awakening Islam: The Politics of Religious Dissent in Contemporary Saudi Arabia.* Trans. by George Holoch. Cambridge, Mass.: Harvard University Press, 2011. p. 373.

Call it what you may, "The Islamic awakening," "al Sahwa al Islamiyya," or simply "Sahwa," the movement described by Stéphane Lacroix was absent from the Saudi Arabian landscape until it emerged in the 1990s. The Sahwa, Lacroix finds, must be regarded as a distinctive form of Islamism, a hybrid of the Muslim Brotherhood and the Wahhabi tradition. True, the Sahwa was preceded by other movements in the Middle East, notably by the Muslim Brotherhood that emerged in Egypt in 1928. The Brotherhood's founder, Hasan al-Banna (1906–1949), created it as an organization to promote the establishment of an Islamic state that would be ruled by Shari'a. The movement grew rapidly and provided crucial support to the Egyptian revolution of July 1952, the one that brought Gamal Abdel Nasser to power.

Lacroix's time framework for this work begins with the late nineteenth century when Muslim reformism first began to appear, but he is primarily interested in the 1960s and the 1970s, a period that witnessed the development of a vast social movement advancing a modern form of Islam throughout the Middle East. His study of Islam is further narrowed to that which occurred in Saudi Arabia in the 1970s when an intellectual class began to show hostility to both Sufism and popular Islam. By Lacroix's account, the intelligentsia became open to Western modes of thinking in the 1970s largely because Saudi Arabia had sent students to foreign universities, at first in Egypt, Lebanon, and Iraq, beginning in the 1940s, and later to Western universities. State bureaucratic administrations co-opted many of the returning university students. The young intelligentsia, whose training had introduced them to liberal movements, consequently became in many cases nationalistic, leftist, socialist, or communist. Lacroix finds it worthy of note that liberalization in some quarters first took the form of questioning classical rules of poetry.

Lacroix began his study convinced that Saudi Arabia remains a blind spot in many Western studies of Islamism. "Although all writers agree," he writes, "that Saudi Arabia is the key to the expansion of Islamist movements in the Middle East, few describe the tenor and methods of the influence." Lacroix thus takes as his task the description and viability of Islam in Saudi Arabia. Saudi Arabia is undoubtedly an exporter of Islam, he reports, but it also has to be seen as the recipient of influences emanating from most currents of nineteenth- and twentieth-century Islamic revivalism. The activist movement inspired by Abd al-Wahhab cannot be ignored. In almost all countries of the Muslim world, Islamism arose and developed outside the state. The converse is true of Saudi Arabia where, from the beginning, Islamism was integrated into the kingdom's official institutions. The situation of the Saudi Islamist movement is thus different from that of most Middle Eastern countries because it is not a question of combating a secular regime that relies on a source of legitimacy other than religion. "What is at issue (in Saudi Arabia) is challenging the monopoly over the divine held by a government based on religion." Yet Islam in Saudi Arabia is a subject of contention not only between the regime and the Islamists but also among the Islamists themselves and the multiplicity of visions that motivate them. Islam is the primary language in which social rivalries and cultural issues are expressed.

When in August 1990 Saddam Hussein attacked Kuwait, the Saudi regime was forced to call upon American troops to protect its territory against a possible Iraqi attack. The resulting presence of foreign troops in the land of Islam's holy places fostered a formidable opposition against the royal family. Lacroix attributes the Islamic awakening largely to the feeling of anger at the American presence. That presence served as a symbol of the moral and political failure of the Saudi system itself, a presence that continues to motivate multiple protests from the intellectual and religious elite alike.

Lacroix's investigation leads him to a study of Wahhabism, which he admits is difficult to define because, in his words, "it is not an unchangeable essence but a tradition in motion subject to interpretation and reinterpretation, possessed of no well-defined characteristics." The founding moment of the Saudi field of power as it exists today, he dates to the pact of 1744 "joining the sword of Muhammad bin Sa'ud to the religious call of the preacher Muhammad bin Abd al-Wahhab." In the words of Sayyid Qutb, "The sovereignty of God will be restored only when there is a pure Islamic state, based on Shari'a alone."

Although written before the Middle East uprisings in the early part of 2011, this densely packed and well-documented book may be considered essential reading for anyone attempting to understand the significant role that the Muslim Brotherhood has played and continues to play throughout the area. From its founding the Muslim Brotherhood has had the dual purpose of fighting foreign occupation and establishing an Islamic state that would apply Shari'a. Several sections of *Awakening Islam* are devoted to the Brotherhood's presence in Saudi Arabia, where it has played an essential role in moral education and, one may say, cultural education generally. The Brotherhood is noted for its creation of institutes and universities and for the establishment of education programs for the children of the Kingdom. Intellectual elites are attracted to its programs. While its leaders do not shy from an exegesis of the Koran and/or from contributions to Islamic jurisprudence, *creed* is recognized as the exclusive province of the Wahhabi ulama.

Given his richly detailed study of the Islamic awakening, Lacroix seems reluctant to draw any conclusion except that "the Saudi Islamists and the Sahwa will remain central actors on the kingdom's political stage for years and possibly decades to come." The reader, however, will recognize the religious ambiguity, complexity, and plasticity of the movement that the author calls "Sahwa" and the continuing danger that Islam presents for the West.

Al-Jabbar, Abd. *Critique of Christian Origins.* A parallel English-Arabic text, edited, translated, and annotated by Gabriel Said Reynolds and Khalil Samir. Provo, Utah: Brigham Young University Press, 2010. Pp. lxxv + 249.

This is a volume in the "Islamic Translation" series sponsored by the Brigham Young University. The treatise presented here is the work of a prominent medieval theologian, Abd al-Jabbar, (c. 930s — d. 1024), who writes to explain the birth and nature of Christianity. His task is to defend the claims of Islamic theology that Jesus was a Muslim prophet when Christians claim that He is God-Incarnate, Lord and Savior, and the founder of a Church. *Critique of Christian Origins* is one of many early Islamic critiques of Christianity. Al-Jabbar writes in what is known as the Mu'tazili style of scholarship. With great confidence in the reliability of human reason, he is convinced that religious claims must meet conventional standards of logic. Thus intellectual reflection on God-given knowledge is indispensable.

Muslims usually begin their historical narrative with the time of the Prophet Muhammad and have little to say about the six hundred years between Jesus and Muhammad. Al-Jabbar is aware that Christians, by contrast, have a well-developed historical narrative that connects them to the life and time of Jesus. Muslim scholars before Abd al-Jabbar who tried to demonstrate the invalidity of Christianity did so only at the level of doctrine, hoping to prove that Christianity is abhorrent to reason. In fact, early Muslim scholars possessed little knowledge of Christian scripture and practice in spite of their considerable knowledge of Christological and Trinitarian debates. In the treatise presented here al-Jabbar takes a different tack insofar as he turns to history to support his argument that Christianity is a human invention and not of divine origin.

The translators in their introduction acknowledge that "It is no easy task to describe the *Qur'an*'s evaluation of Christianity for the precise

historical context of the *Qur'an*'s origins is far from clear." The *Qur'an*
implies that Christians belittle God with their statements about Christ
by calling him "The Son of God." Islam lays claim to Jesus as its own,
and He is often presented as one in a chain of prophets from Adam to
Muhammad. In the *Qur'an* Jesus seems to be singled out above all
prophets. As Reynolds and Samir in their introduction express the doctrine, "His birth without a father at the beginning of his life and his
ascension into heaven at its end are extraordinary only inasmuch as
they reflect God's miraculous intervention. They do not redound to
Jesus' nature."

In establishing Muhammad's character as a true prophet, Al-Jabbar
argues that Muhammad's book, the *Qur'an*, discloses information that
could only have come from God. As the translators summarize his position, "To Abd al-Jabbar, Muhammad's rejection of Christianity is an
indication of the divine origin of his knowledge. No one—especially
not a simple and uneducated Arab, as al-Jabbar holds Muhammad to
be—would have the audacity to reject an ancient religion, a religion
cherished by many people and powerful nations, unless he had divine
authority to do so." It is al-Jabbar's claim that he, al-Jabbar, knows
Christianity to be invalid because of his study of it, but Muhammad
could only have known it as revealed by God. Al-Jabbar believes that
Muhammad's "miraculous knowledge of Christianity" is evidence that
he is a true prophet. Still, he has to address the charge that a true
prophet would not have shed blood as Muhammad did or have multiple
wives and concubines as Muhammad did. This he attempts by claiming
that the prophets of Israel, whom the Christians venerate, did as much.

Al-Jabbar is particularly harsh in his treatment of the Apostle Paul,
whom he accuses of Romanizing Christianity and of Constantine for
the imposition of Christianity by bloodshed. He is convinced that
Christianity is not a valid expression of the religion of Christ but a con-
tinuation of pagan Roman practices.

Besides making a rare text available in English, one of the merits
of this volume is that the translators introduce the layman to the vast
Islamic literature that arose in the tenth and eleventh centuries as
Islamic scholars grappled not only with Christian theologians but with
Islamic philosophers as well.

Jon McGinnis. *Avicenna.* Oxford: Oxford University Press, 2010. pp. xiv + 300. $99.00 (cloth); $29.95 (paper).

This is a valuable work not merely because it is an impressive study of the philosophy of Avicenna but because it places him in the context of his time. McGinnis describes at some length the classical philosophical curriculum which formed Avicenna and the complex Islamic intellectual milieu in which he functioned at the time. Nothing much has changed in the thousand years since his death. The curriculum which launched Avicenna still prevails in those institutions of higher learning that still take philosophy seriously and the internal Islamic quarrels that contributed to his distress have yet to be resolved. By the time of Avicenna, there were two schools of Islam, the Mu'tazilites, who rejected a literal interpretation of the Qur'an, and the Ash'arites, who favored a literal interpretation. The latter came to dominate Sunni Islam.

Born in 980 in Bukhara in what is now modern day Uzbekistan, Avicenna produced before his death at age 58 nearly 300 works, including no less than three (extant) *summas.* His crowning achievement is undoubtedly his monumental encyclopedia known as the *Cure.* His last years were spent in the central mountain country of modern Iran where he had been forced to flee after having been imprisoned in 1023.

In his autobiography, he relates that by the age of ten, he had memorized the entire Qur'an as well as many works of Arabic literature. Before the age of sixteen he had read Porphyry's *Isagoge,* Euclid's *Elements* and Ptolemy's *Almagest,* and had studied Indian arithmetic and Islamic law. He confesses that he had read Aristotle's *Metaphysics* forty times without comprehension before he discovered al-Farabi's short treatise on the aims of metaphysics which opened the work to his understanding. By age seventeen he had so mastered the medical texts of his day, and given that his hands-on care for the sick had given him clinical experience, he was called to advise physicians at the court of al-Mansur.

In his exposition of Avicenna's philosophy, McGinnis follows the order in which classical philosophy was traditionally taught in the schools of Athens and Alexandria, beginning with logic, followed by natural science, psychology, metaphysics, and finally ethics. The bulk of the present volume is devoted to Avicenna's psychology and metaphysics, with the section on psychology divided into two parts, Part I, dealing with that which is common to sentient life, and Part II devoted to the human intellect. Avicenna's analysis of the abstractive power of the human intellect and of intellectual memory leads him to affirm the immaterial character of the human soul. Given the soul's immaterial being, he infers that it is capable of existing apart from the body. Thus, with the introduction of an immaterial intellect, Avicenna has moved beyond the science of physics and into the realm of metaphysics.

Metaphysics he defines as the science of existence *qua* existence. Given Avicenna's acknowledgment of a real distinction between essence and existence and his recognition of the contingent existence of the beings of sense experience, he reasons to a Necessary Existent, the cause of the existence of things. A discussion of the attributes of the Necessary Existent follows. There quickly arises the question, "Was the world created in time or did it exist from eternity?" Avicenna is led to defend the eternity thesis.

McGinnis makes it clear that Avicenna's work is important not only in itself, and for the value it retains for contemporary metaphysical discussion, but for the influence it had on Aquinas, Scotus, and Maimonides. A detailed examination of that influence was not the intent of the present volume, but one can hope that McGinnis may one day undertake it with his admirable thoroughness.

Chérif, Mustapha. *Islam and the West: A Conversation with Jacques Derrida*, originally published as *L'Islam et l'occident*, trans. by Teresa L. Fagan. Chicago: University of Chicago Press, 2008. xxii + 114 pp. Cloth, $19.00.

Months before his death in 2004, Jacques Derrida participated in a free-ranging, public discussion with Mustapha Chérif on the topic "Islam and the West." Organized by Chérif, a professor of philosophy and Islamic studies at the University of Algiers, the discussion took place in Paris at the Institut du Monde Arabe. We have in book form Chérif's account of the conversation, with some direct quotations but not a verbatim transcript of the discussion.

Although diagnosed that same day with terminal illness, Derrida honored his commitment to the dialogue with Chérif. He had multiple reasons for doing so. Derrida, like Chérif, was a native of the Maghreb. Born in Algiers in 1930 of Jewish parents, Derrida lived through the tremulous years of the French disengagement and later, after studying in France, became a public intellectual, with considerable influence in France and perhaps even greater influence in North America. Derrida is associated with the post-modernist, literary movement known as "deconstruction" and is acclaimed both as its founder and chief proponent. One will look in vain for a simple coherent definition of deconstruction. Although rooted in linguistics and in the study of how words convey meaning, it may reflect more of a mood or of an attitude than a rational methodology. However defined, it is a thoroughgoing critique of the certainties that have animated Western culture since antiquity. Not only skeptical of received wisdom, it is skeptical of all authority, civil and ecclesiastical, and even of the possibility of truth, given that there can be no objective understanding of reality.

In the course of the dialogue, Chérif tells us that Islamic scholars, unlike Samuel P. Huntington and Bernard Lewis, reject the notion that there is a clash of cultures between Islam and the West. The eradication of the opposition between Islam and the West, especially within the divided unity of Mediterranean civilization, is one of Derrida's abiding objectives. With Chérif, he speaks of the northern and southern shores of the Mediterranean basin as two halves of a geographical, ethnic, and cultural unity. Chérif insists that what is called the classical West is properly understood as Judeo-Islamic-Christian, not Greco-Roman or Judeo-Christian. He goes on to say that Islam is not a culture but a religion. The silent majorities of moderate Muslims, he is convinced, condemn the use of religion for political purposes and are opposed to the misguided and fanatical extremists who act in the name of Islam.

The conversation moved from a discussion of Islam to broader questions of secularism and democracy, to politics and religion and how the former manipulates the latter. Derrida is at the forefront of a movement that calls for "universal democracy," a democracy that is not connected to citizenship, to territory, to a nation, to a state, or to religion. He calls for new international law and international institutions capable of imposing their decisions. The transformation of international law obviously implies a revision of the traditional notion of sovereignty. Given Derrida's idealized version of universal democracy, there would no longer be any sovereign nation-state. In his proposed universal civilization, technical and economic transformation would follow the political, becoming the exclusive property of none. The universal democracy Derrida seeks, since it is not connected to citizenship or to territoriality, would remove a xenophobic exclusion of the "different other." Such he believes is the necessary condition for freedom of speech, for exchange, for dialogue, for mutual understanding.

In keeping with the thrust of deconstruction, Derrida conveniently ignores the Hellenic and Christian sources of Western democracy and the culture that supports it. Chérif, for his part, is obliged to ignore the history of Islam and the texts in the Koran and in the Hadiths that through the centuries have inspired the jihad and the violence that Chérif so rightly condemns. Although Pierre Manent probably did not have Derrida in mind when he published *Democracy without Nations? The Fate of Self-Government in Europe*, that book serves as an antidote to the visionary universal democracy proclaimed in this volume.

Shahîd, Irfan. *Byzantium and the Arabs in the Sixth Century, Volume II, Part 2: Economic, Social, and Cultural History.* Washington, DC: Dumbarton Oaks Research Library and Collection, 2009. pp. xxiii + 391. (Cloth), $50.00.

This is one in a series of six volumes devoted to the study of Arab-Byzantium relations in late antiquity. Volume II can stand alone as a study of the Ghassânid, a *foederati* or a tribal alliance that migrated from the south of the Arab peninsula to the Diocese of Oriens (Bil~d al-Sh~m) in the fifth century. Influenced by the gravitational pull of Byzantium in its tripartite structure of Romanitas, Hellenism, and Christianity, they created a unique and mature Christian culture in the Diocese of Oriens, in the shadow of the Roman Empire, a culture which, Shahîd reminds his reader, obtained only once in Arabic history. Sadly it came to an end in the seventh century with the Islamic conquest, but "Its flame," Shahîd tells us, "independently rekindled some twelve centuries later, has been flickering fitfully and intermittently in present day Lebanon."

Shahîd implies that historians of Oriental Christianity either tend to neglect its Arabic element or vaguely treat it. Arabic identity, he insists, contributed to the diversity of early Christian culture. The Ghassânid, profoundly influenced by their Christian faith, set about building churches and monasteries; their king even presided over church councils. Christianity opened the *foederati* to the larger outside Hellenic and Roman worlds. The Arabic king, Abgar the Great, is credited with making Edessa the spiritual capital of the Semite Christian Orient, just as Antioch had been established as its counterpart for the Greco-Roman Orient.

The Ghassânid military when employed by Byzantium defended the Diocese of Oriens, the Holy Lands, and fought the wars of the empire in the East. They and other *foederati* performed non-military duties in times of peace, just as the Roman legionaries did in peacetime. Of the Ghassānid military, Shahîd speaks of their twin virtues—courage and endurance in battle. This was professionalized and sophisticated by the Roman element when the Ghassānid were trained to fight in the Roman manner. The new Romano-Arab warrior was inspired by the most powerful component of Byzantium, Christianity. The wars that the Ghassānid were called upon to fight became spiritualized and became more meaningful by being harnessed to the ideals of their religious faith as they undertook religious war in defense of the Christian Roman Empire, its Holy Land, and in campaigns against the Persians and the Lakhmid Arabs.

In their professional, social, cultural, and spiritual life the Ghassānid were intense in the profession of their Christian faith. That faith may have set them apart, but unlike the German tribes who were *foederati* in the Roman Occident, the Ghassānid were related ethnically and linguistically to the larger Arab component in the demographic landscape of Oriens.

Of all the venues of cultural life in the Ghassānid city, the monastery was the most important. By the sixth century, the monastery had emerged not only as a place for the *imitatio Christi*, but also as a cultural center where literary pursuits were encouraged. The monasteries promoted the creation of libraries and study groups, and their members provided instruction for both children and adults. Transcribing and reproducing manuscripts, both secular and ecclesiastic, and translating texts from the Greek into Syriac became common practice. Not only that, the monasteries produced original creative literary works. Sometimes the translations went the other way, from the Syriac into the Greek. The great figure in the golden period of Syriac literature, the fourth-century Ephrem of Edessa, was translated into Greek. His metrical compositions, the madrashe, are said to have influenced hymnography in the Diocese of Oriens.

Worthy of note is that much of the Ghassānid achievement—economic, social, and cultural—persisted under the new Umayyad Caliphate after the Ghassānid were defeated by the Muslims in the battle of Yarmāk (636). Many of the traits that Shahîd attributes to the Ghassānid are to be found in contemporary Islam, notably its spiritual intensity and its tendency to refer all things to Allah, similar to the *milites Christi* of the Ghassānid.

Whereas many volumes produced under the patronage of Islamic study centers at major universities and published by prestigious university presses seem little more than propaganda for one Islamic cause or another, this work has the mark of honest and probing scholarship. A short review cannot do justice to Byzantium and the Arabs in the Sixth Century or to the scholarship on which it is based. Suffice it to say, the book opens the reader to a little-known but intensely interesting period in Arabic history.

Lewis, Bernard. *Faith and Power: Religion and Politics in the Middle East.* New York: Oxford University Press, 2010. pp. xxi + 208.

Although the book has the appearance of a monograph, it is a collection of essays, unpublished lectures, and excerpts from Lewis's other writings. *Faith and Power* is reminiscent of Hilaire Belloc's *Europe and the Faith* (1920). Both Belloc and Lewis in much of their work may be regarded as public intellectuals. Both bring to their topics extensive historical knowledge in their effort to take the measure of the present in the light of the past: Belloc addressed the unifying element of what was then commonly identified as Christendom; Lewis focuses on the common Islamic faith of today's Middle East.

In passing, Lewis reviews fourteen centuries of conflict between Islam and Christianity, "rival faiths," he calls them, "with alternate messages to mankind." For most of the Middle Ages, Islam represented a mortal danger to Europe. That changed with the West's successful defense of Vienna and the French occupation of Egypt under Napoleon in 1798. It was the French conquest of Egypt that initially brought Western influence to the very center of the Middle East. From the Islamic point of view, the Christian enemy had somehow managed to establish a transitory military supremacy. Eventually the heartlands of Islam became subject to the influence, dominance, and, at times, direct rule of Europe's imperial powers, Britain, France, and Russia who deprived most of the Islamic world of sovereignty. Foreign rule was seen as tyranny, and the overriding political aim of the Islamic states of the Middle East was to end it, to regain independence.

Islamic *polity*, Lewis reminds his reader, defines itself by religion, that is, as a society in which identity and allegiance are determined by the acceptance of a common faith. The distinction between church and state, spiritual and temporal, ecclesiastical and lay, is a Christian concept that has had no analogue in Islamic history. Muslims typically are very conscious of their identity. They know who they are and what they want, and, Lewis adds, "a quality that many in the West seem to a very large extent to have lost." In an Islamic state there is in principle no law other than Shari'a, the holy law of Islam. In the traditional order, the only lawgivers were of the ulema, doctors of the holy law who were at once jurists and theologians. The Prophet Muhammad, as head of state, not only promulgated the law but also applied and enforced it. His successors did the same.

Lewis makes a distinction between Islamic fundamentalism and Islam itself and makes the point that most Muslims are not fundamentalists, and further, that most fundamentalists are not terrorists. "At no point," he writes, "do the basic texts of Islam enjoin terrorism and murder. At no point do they ever consider the random slaughter of uninvolved bystanders." Yet, no one can deny that Islamic terrorism is a reality. Lewis is forced to acknowledge calls to violence on the part of Muslim authorities. The 1998 "Declaration of the World Islamic Front for the Jihad against Jews and Crusaders" was supposedly signed by Osama bin Laden and leaders of militant Islamist groups in Egypt, Pakistan, and Bangladesh. The document holds that "To kill Americans and their allies, both civil and military, is an individual duty of every Muslim who is able, in any country where this is possible." Even so, Lewis explains, "The fundamentalist aim is to end the corruption of Islamic society and restore the God-given holy law of Islam." That, of course, is not characteristic of Islam as a whole. In Lewis's account, two main ideas compete at present in the Middle East region, with two diagnoses of the sickness of the society and two prescriptions for its cure. One of them is the modernist, usually secularist approach, the idea that it is possible and necessary for the Islamic lands to become part of modern civilization; or put frankly, the region is backward and impoverished because it clings to outmoded ideas and institutions. The remedy for the modernist is that of Kemal Ataturk in Turkey. The other solution, governed by a revulsion against Western civilization, is that of the fundamentalist who holds that what is wrong in the Muslim world is that Muslims have not been faithful to their inherited traditions. The remedy is to return to the roots of authentic Islam.

Where does Europe stand now?, Lewis asks. "From the first irruption of Muslim Arabs in the seventh century to the second Turkish Muslim siege of Vienna in 1683, the pattern of relationship between [European Christendom and Middle Eastern Islam] was one of Muslim advance and Christian retreat, and the issue of the struggle was the possession of Europe." For the greater part of their history, Muslims had been accustomed to a position of supremacy and dominance. Muslims had ruled, unbelievers had submitted, and the leaders of the infidels, both at home and abroad, had recognized the supremacy of Islam. In the broad realms of the Islamic empires, the Christian populations had either embraced Islam or accepted a position of tolerated subordination.

Will Islam be successful in its third attempt to take over Europe? It is not impossible, Lewis believes. Muslims have certain clear advantages. The growth of Western self-doubt and self-criticism provides fertile ground. Muslims have fervor and conviction, which in most Western countries is weak or lacking. They have loyalty and discipline, but most of all they have demography on their side. The combination of natural population increases and uncontrolled immigration have produced major population changes which could lead in the foreseeable future to significant Islamic majorities in some European nations with corresponding political power. While their political impact is limited at present, the children of the newcomers will be native-born. It will not be possible in the long run to deny them citizenship. The consequence of a population many millions strong of Muslims born and educated in Western Europe will have immense and unpredictable consequences for Europe. Christianity itself poses no threat to Islam. "While Christian power," Lewis writes, "might at times have seemed a threat, Christian religion was never, and the very idea was an absurdity. How could a Muslim be attracted to an earlier, abrogated version of his own religion, and moreover one professed by subject peoples whom he had conquered and over whom he held sway."

Faith and Power is suffused with Lewis's broad historical knowledge and the insight that comes from years of reflection. Given Lewis's somewhat romantic interpretation of its past, Islam could not want a more steadfast apologist. Lewis is convinced that once the dictators of the Middle East are eliminated, there can be a rapprochement between Islam and the West or at least a constructive engagement. "Let's talk to them, let's get together to see what we can do." After all Islam has a certain appeal to the left-wing, anti-American element in Europe. In this and in his more technical treatises, Lewis's work cannot be discounted. Yet Ignaz Goldhizer's *Introduction to Islamic Theology* (1905) remains a valuable source for anyone interested in the origin and development of Islamic thought over the centuries, a book available in English translation from Princeton University Press (1981).

Brague, Rémi. *The Legend of the Middle Ages:*
Philosophical Explorations of Medieval Christianity,
Judaism, and Islam. Trans. by Lydia G. Cochrane.
Chicago: University of Chicago Press, 2009. pp. xi + 287.
Cloth, $35.00; £24.00.

The premise that animates this enquiry is that the Middle Ages is a
period of history that has something to tell us about ourselves. In an
autobiographical note, Brague tells the reader how his classical studies led him out of his early work on Plato and Aristotle to a serious
study of the Middle Ages and a professorship in Arabic medieval
philosophy. Any French man or woman who studies medieval philosophy is perforce an autodidact, given the absence of medieval studies in the French curriculum even at the university level. Many
American readers will remember that Etienne Gilson founded his
influential Pontifical Institute of Mediaeval Studies not in France but
in Toronto.

Brague opens with a set of distinctions rarely encountered in contemporary literature, i.e., between theology in Christianity and Kalam
in Islam, between philosophy in Christianity and Falsafa in Islam, elaborating on the terms and the difference in understanding they make.

Addressing the genesis of European culture, Brague acknowledges,
"Europe borrowed its nourishment, first from the Greco-Roman world
that preceded it, then from the world of Arabic culture that developed
in parallel with it, and finally from the Byzantine world. It is from the
Arabic world, in particular, that Europe gained the texts of Aristotle,
Galen, and many others that, once translated from the Arabic into Latin,
fed the twelfth-century renaissance." Later the Byzantine world provided the original version of those same texts, which permitted close study
and alimented the flowering of scholasticism." Where would Thomas
Aquinas have been, he asks, if he had not found a worthy adversary in

Averroes? What would Duns Scotus have contributed if he had not taken Avicenna as a point of departure?

Islamic philosophy is usually seen as beginning with al-Kindi, around the ninth century and ending with Averroes around the twelfth century. No one contests the fact that Muslims continue to think after Averroes, but what remains to be defined is to what extent that thought can be called "philosophy." There are in history highly respectable works that one would never call philosophical but which we would nevertheless describe as "wisdom literature" or "thoughts." Heidegger, Brague tells us, would place "thought" on a higher plane than philosophy. Brague is particularly sensitive to the broader cultural context in which philosophy is developed. He finds that the opinions generally admitted within a given community provide the basis on which philosophy is built. Those opinions are historically conditioned, and they come in the final analysis, he maintains, from the legislator of the community. All medieval works were affected by this phenomenon. Within Christianity, revelation is the all-important communal bond. "Muslim and Jewish revelations, which are presented as laws, do not pose the same problems as Christian revelation." Reconciling religion and philosophy is an epistemological problem in Christianity and may even be a psychological one, but in Islam and Judaism reconciling religion and revelation is primarily a political problem. Unlike Islam and Judaism, Christianity includes the Magisterium of the Church, whose teaching is granted authority in the intellectual domain.

The institutionalization of philosophy, Brague points out, took place under the tutelage of the Church and remains exclusively European. There was indeed something like higher education in all three Mediterranean worlds, but the teaching of philosophy at the university level existed neither in the Muslim world nor in Jewish communities. Jewish philosophy and Muslim philosophy were private enterprises. It is usual to compare the great philosophers of each tradition, for example, Averroes, Maimonides, and Thomas Aquinas, but the difference is that Thomas was one of many engaged in the same corporate activity, standing out, it is true, among countless obscure figures. Within Islam there is no corpus of canonical texts that lend themselves to *disputatio*. To illustrate the difference, Brague remarks, "You can be a perfectly competent rabbi or imam without ever having studied philosophy. In contrast, a philosophical background is a necessary part of the basic equipment of the Christian theologian." Leo Strauss, acknowledging the status of philosophy in Christianity, on the one hand, and in Islam and Judaism, on the other, regards the institutionalization of philosophy as a double-edged sword. The official acknowledgment of philosophy in the Christian world made philosophy subject to ecclesiastical supervision, whereas the precarious position of philosophy in the Islamic-Jewish world guaranteed its private character and therewith its inner freedom from supervision. Brague contests Strauss on this point as would any Catholic scholar who has pursued a philosophical vocation.

Brague offers a chapter on the importance of the study of nature. From the point of view of Ibn Khaldun (1332–1406), "The problems of physics are of no interest to us in our religious affairs or in our livelihoods. Therefore we must leave them alone." Physics, he held, must not bother us because it cannot be applied to the two domains that are truly important to us: this life and the life to come. Averroes, by contrast, will say that the study of nature is obligatory because a knowledge of nature leads to a knowledge of its Author. The real goal is to know God, the Creator, through His creation. Thomas in the *Summa contra Gentiles* devotes two chapters to the pertinence of the study of nature for theology and suggests that scientific knowledge of nature has the added effect of freeing one from the superstitions of astrology. Brague adds, "Thomas's intention (among others) is not far from that of Epicurus, who sought to calm human anguish, one of the most dangerous types which is anguish before celestial phenomena."

A succeeding chapter addresses the difference between Christianity and Islam from the Muslim point of view. Ibn Khaldun is again taken as an authoritative source. In Ibn Khaldun's view, as presented by Brague, within the Muslim community the holy war is a religious duty because of the universalism of the Muslim mission and the obligation to convert all non-Muslims to Islam either by persuasion or by force. In consequence the caliphate and royal authority are rightly united in Islam so that the person in charge can devote his available strength to both objectives at the same time. "The other religious groups," Ibn

Khaldun finds, "do not have a universal mission and the holy war is not a religious duty to them, save only for purposes of defense. It has thus come about that the person in charge of religious affairs in other religious groups is not concerned with power politics. Royal authority comes to those who have it by accident, and in some way that has nothing to do with religion and not because they are under obligation to gain power over other nations." Holy war exists only within Islam and furthermore, Ibn Khaldun insists, it is imposed by Shari'a.

Its theological warrant aside, Brague asks, how is jihad viewed from the vantage point of Islam's greatest philosophers? He puts the question to three Aristotelians, al Farabi (c. 870–950), Avicenna (980–1037), and Averroes (1126–1198), all of whom profess belief in Islam. All three permit the waging of holy war against those who refuse Islam: al Farabi and Averroes against the Christians, Avicenna against the pagans he encounters in Persia. Al Farabi, who lived and wrote in the lands where the enemy was the Byzantine empire, draws up a list of seven justifications for war, including the right to conduct war in order to acquire something that the state desires to have but is in the possession of others, the right of combat against people for whom it is better that they serve but who refuse the yoke of slavery, and the right to wage holy war to force people to accept what is better for them if they do not recognize it spontaneously. Averroes, writing in the farthest Western part of the Islamic empire, approves without reservation the slaughter of dissidents, calling for the total elimination of a people whose continued existence might harm the state. Avicenna condones conquest and readily grants the leader of his ideal society the right to annihilate those who called to truth reject it. In general the philosophers express no remorse about widespread bloodletting, and Brague offers some additional examples. Al Farabi has nothing to say about the murder of "bestial" men. Avicenna suggests that the religious skeptic should be tortured until he admits the difference between the true and the not true and is penitent. And Averroes advocated the elimination of the mentally handicapped.

Although the book has some appendices and 43 pages of supporting notes, the last chapter of *The Legend of the Middle Ages* is entitled, "Was Averroes a 'Good Guy'?" One might add, in spite of the fact that he condoned the extermination of the handicapped, favored the execution of heretics, and sanctioned what today is called ethnic cleansing. Moral issues aside, Thomas Aquinas accused him of being more the corrupter of Aristotelian philosophy than its interpreter.

Karsh, Efraim. *Islamic Imperialism: A History.* New
Haven: Yale University Press, 2007. 284 pp. Cloth, $30;
paper, $17.

In his epilogue to this volume, Karsh concludes, "Though tempered
and qualified in different places and at different times, the Islamic
longing for unfettered suzerainty has never disappeared, and has resur-
faced in our own day with a vengeance. He goes on to say, "If today
America is reviled in the Muslim world, it is not because of its specific policies but because as the preeminent world power it blocks the
final realization of this same age-old dream of regaining the glory of
the caliphate."

In successive chapters Karsh provides a fascinating account of
Islam from the Warrior Prophet to Osama bin Laden, providing the
reader with an historical survey of the Umayyad Dynasty, the Abbasid
Dynasty, and finally that of the Ottoman Empire. The first Islamic
dynasty was that of the Umayyads (661–750). Although overthrown by
the Abbasid caliphate in 750, the Umayyads were nevertheless to rule
Spain for more than 300 years. During those years the Umayyads
achieved, by all accounts, a level of political, economic, and cultural
greatness, unknown elsewhere in the Islamic world; in Karsh's judgment, largely because they were divided from the rest of the Islamic
world. The indigenous Christians remained loyal to the Church and to
their native culture and language. By the end of the Umayyad era less
than ten percent of the empire's subjects had adopted Islam. The
Umayyads, in Karsh's judgment, were first and foremost imperial mon-
archs for whom Islam was but a means to shore up their credentials.
Islam was a handy façade behind which they could fully enjoy the fruits
of their imperial expansion accomplished in the name of Allah. The
Abbasids, no less secular than the Umayyads, held the caliphate until it
was destroyed by the Mongol invasion of 1258. Under the Abbasids the
basis for the authority of the caliphate shifted from Arab nationality to

international membership in the community of believers. The Ottomans, who began their rule at the beginning of the fourteenth century, at the peak of their power had conquered southeastern Europe, the Middle East, and North Africa and were to rule in the name of Allah for centuries before the empire disintegrated at the time of World War I.

Karsh interprets the history of Islam in the light of its steadfast goal of "world domination," the creation of a universal ummah. He defends his perspective by citing the declared objectives of Islamic leaders through the centuries, from the Prophet himself, through Saladin, Khomeini, and finally Osama bin Laden. Mohammad, in his farewell address (March 632), told his followers: "I was ordered to fight all men until they say, 'There is no god but Allah.'" Saladin, in January 1189, repeated the mandate: "I will cross this sea to their islands to pursue them until there remains no one on the face of the earth who does not acknowledge Allah." Ayatollah Ruhollah Khomeini, in 1979, similarly inspired his followers: "We will export our revolution throughout the world. . . until the calls, 'there is no god but Allah and Mohammad is the messenger of Allah' are echoed all over the world." And Osama bin Laden, within the memory of most, proclaimed: "I was ordered to fight the people until they say there is no god but Allah, and his prophet Mohammad." It cannot be denied, as Karsh points out, that as a universal religion, Islam envisages a global political order in which all humankind will live under Muslim rule and the law of Shari'a, either as believers or subject communities. In order to achieve this goal the House of Islam insists that it is incumbent on all free male adult Muslims to carry out an uncompromising struggle in the path of Allah, or jihad. Those parts of the world that have not been conquered are to be considered permanent battlegrounds. Karsh reminds his reader that Mohammad initially devised the concept of *jihad*, "exertion in the path of Allah," as a means to entice his local followers to raid Meccan caravans and thus, Karsh comments, "instantaneously transformed a common tribal practice into a supreme religious duty and the primary vehicle for the spread of Islam through the ages."

Karsh is insistent upon his interpretative key to the rise and fall of the House of Islam. "No matter how hard the caliphs professed their commitment to the pursuit of a holy war against the

unbelievers, theirs was a straightforward act of empire building."
Karsh challenges the view that there is or need be a "clash of civilizations" between Islam and the West. With some justification he
can say that throughout its history the Islamic faith did not prevent
Muslims from appropriating the intellectual property as well as the
material holdings of other cultures and religions. The absorption of
the conquered civilizations was often thorough and comprehensive.
Indian medicine, mathematics, and astronomy were studied; Iranian
administrative techniques borrowed; so too Iranian social, artistic,
and economic traditions were adopted. The greatest borrowing was
undoubtedly the wholesale incorporation of Hellenic science and
philosophy.

Be that as it may, Karsh does not deny the Islamic threat to
Europe. Uncontrolled immigration and population projections
point to Islamic domination in Europe by the end of the present
century, given Europe's unwillingness to defend its inherited culture. The drive for world domination remains an integral part of the
Islamic creed. "The fuel of Islamic imperialism remains as volatile
as ever," Karsh concedes. In spite of the growing adoption of
Western ideals and practices, Islam has not abandoned the notion
of Allah's universal sovereignty. Karsh finds considerable sympa-
thy throughout the Muslim world for the motives, if not the deeds,
of those who carried out the 9/11 attacks and the London and
Madrid bombings.

Karsh brings his study to a close with this judgment: "Only when
the political elites of the Middle East and the Muslim world reconcile themselves to the reality of state nationalism, foreswear pan-
Arab and pan-Islamic dreams and make Islam a matter of private
faith rather than a tool of political ambition will the inhabitants of
these regions at last be able to look forward to a better future free of
would-be Saladins." That may be true, but it is also true that with the
eclipse of Christianity and the threatened loss of national and cultural identity among the member states of the European Union,
Saladin's dream of conquering the Continent may yet be accomplished, not by military means but through population growth favor-
able to Islam.

Donner, Fred M. *Muhammad and the Believers: At the Origins of Islam.* Cambridge: Harvard University Press, 2010. pp. xviii + 280. (Cloth) $25.95.

Donner makes the case that a proper understanding of Islam requires that it be examined in its beginnings against the background of religious trends that prevailed in the Near East in late antiquity, that is, from the third to the seventh century. He admits that the task is a challenge to the professional historian. Throughout his treatment of the origins of Islam he finds it necessary to distinguish between the "traditional narratives" and the hard evidence available to the historian. The traditional narratives he uses sparingly and with caution. The most important source of information about the early Community of Believers, he holds, is the Qur'an itself.

The early followers of Mohammad thought of themselves as a "Community of Believers," open to all who believed in the oneness of God and in righteous living. Donner refers to its early years as its ecumenical period when Jews and Christians (Monophysites, probably) could be found among its members. It was later tradition, about a century after Muhammad's time, that his followers began to identify themselves as Muslims, i.e., as those who submit. The Qur'an, as a written document, was not available to the early Believers. It did not yet exist. Donner finds that the revelations which comprise the Qur'an did not take the form of a written book until about twenty years after the Prophet's death. It was then that the scattered written and unwritten parts of the revelations were collected by an editorial committee and compiled in definite written form.

The Qur'an, in addressing people whom it calls "Believers," sets out their basic commitments. They believed, first of all, in the oneness of God, in a strict monotheism. They are mindful and obedient to God's will, a God who created all things and gave us life. They believed that on the Day of Judgment, the last day, the whole of mankind will be brought before God and in a final judgment consigned either to paradise or to the torments of hell. Most beliefs flowed from the centrality of the belief that God is one, not Trinitarian. Believers also held that God uses angels to intervene in mundane affairs when it is His will that they do so. Satan is recognized as a fallen angel. Sin requires atonement. Theft, adultery, infanticide, bearing false witness, and disobeying the Prophet are proscribed. Someone guilty of sin was enjoined to pray or offer a *zakat*, a fine or payment in exchange for Muhammad's prayer that the sinner may be purified.

Mere intellectual acceptance of these key doctrines is not enough. One also has to live properly. One is obliged to help the less fortunate and must engage in regular prayer. Ritual prayer is prescribed for the two ends of the day. The mandate prescribing five clearly defined times for prayer occurred a century after Muhammad's death. Jihad is also an integral part of Islamic belief. It is an activist commitment to work in the cause of God. Donner finds its source in Qur'an 8.65, where the Prophet instructs Believers to fight against unbelief and even to "make great slaughter in the earth" in the struggle against unbelievers. Chapter nine of the Qur'an begins with a passage ordering the Believers to capture and to kill unbelievers by every means, but then, Donner notes, it pulls back rather abruptly and commands that unbelievers be allowed to go unharmed if they repent or if they ask the Believers for protection. Protection required the payment of a special tax, *dhimma*.

The story of Islam, as Donner constructs it, begins with Muhammad's consolidation of political power over Medina, his justification of raiding parties, his conquest and occupation of Mecca and the town of Ta'rf in western Arabia, and his organized military expeditions in the north against Tabuk. Once he achieved sufficient power he dispensed with the policy of making alliances with pagan tribes, something previously necessary in his struggle with Mecca. He announced a new policy of non-cooperation with polytheists; they were to be attacked and forced to acknowledge God's oneness. By the end of Muhammad's life, the Believers were not merely a religion with an emphasis on God but a militant pietistic movement bent on aggressively searching out and destroying what its members considered practices odious to God. Following the death of Muhammad the Islamic conquests lasted, with various interruptions, for roughly a century and carried the Believers as far as Spain and India.

The expansion of the Community of Believers and the struggle for leadership occupies the greater part of this volume and concludes with Donner's account of the emergence of Islam under the Umayyads. Donner reminds his readers that the Qur'an provides no direct information on the expansionist movement. Here, he says, one must rely on the traditional narratives which, as a professional historian, he finds "very problematic." Given the clarity of his prose, one may hope that he plans a second volume carrying the story forward. Like Ignaz Goldziher's classic work, *Introduction to Islamic Theology and Law,* written a century ago, this book has the ring of truth where so many of the volumes recently published by university presses seem partisan or merely apologetic works. A not insignificant merit of *Muhammad and the Believers* is the appendix wherein Donner provides his notes and an extensive guide for further reading.

Endnotes

Introduction

1   Etienne Gilson, *The Unity of Philosophical Experience* (New York: Charles Scribner's Sons, 1937), p. vii.
2   Gilson, *Unity*, p. 317.

The Loss of Maritain's America

1   *New York Times*, September 14, 2011, B 6.
2   Jacques Maritain. *Reflections on America* (New York; Charles Scribner's Sons, 1958).
3   Ibid., p.162.
4   Will Herberg, *Protestant, Catholic, Jew* (New York: Doubleday, 1955).
5   Cf. Barbara Ward. Faith and Freedom (New York: W.W. Norton, 1954).
6   Friedrich von Hayek, *The Constitution of Liberty* (Chicago: University of Chicago Press, 1960). Republished in 2011 by the University of Chicago Press, in what it calls the "Definitive Edition."
7   Friedrich von Hayek, *The Road to Serfdom* (Chicago: University of Chicago Press, 1944).
8   Ibid., p. 4.
9   von Hayek, *The Constitution of Liberty*, p. 349.
10 Ibid., p. 210.
11 Ibid., p. 49.
12 Ibid., p. 48.
13 A recent example is Pope Benedict's reflection on the role which the Church played in the unification of Italy. Cf. "Pope Reminds Italy of Its Catholic Identity: Reflections on the 150th Anniversary of Il Risorgimento," as reported by Zenit.org, 3/16/11.

Maritain in the Company of His Peers

1   Jacques Maritain, *The Degrees of Knowledge*, trans. from the 4th French edition by G. B. Phelan (New York: Charles Scribner's Sons, 1959), p. 17.
2   Cf. the widely used textbook by Ernest Nagel, *The Structure of Science: Problems in the Logic of Scientific Explanation* (New York: Harcourt, Brace and World, 1961). Also *Sovereign Reason* (Glencoe, Ill: Free Press, 1954).
3   Donald and Idella Gallagher, *The Achievement of Jacques and Raïssa Maritain: A Bibliography, 1906–1961* (Garden City, NY: Doubleday, 1962), p. 16.
4   Gallagher, op. cit., p. 11.
5   T. S. Eliot, *The Idea of a Christian Society* (London: Faber, 1939).
6   *Washington Post*, April 29, 1973.
7   Gallagher, op. cit., p. 26.

8   Jacques Maritain, *De l'Église du Christ*, trans. by Joseph W. Evans (*On the Church of Christ: The Person of the Church and Her Personnel*) (Notre Dame, Ind.: University of Notre Dame Press, 1973).

9   *Le Paysan de la Garonne* (Paris: Desclee de Brouwer, 1966).

10   Ibid., p. 111.

11   Ibid., p. 138.

12   Ibid., p. 167.

13   Ibid.

14   Ibid., p. 168.

15   Ibid., p. 241.

16   Promulgated June 16, 2000, with the approval of John Paul II and signed by Joseph Cardinal Ratzinger, Prefect of the Congregation for the Doctrine of the Faith.

17   Ibid., p. 14.

18   Cf. *Politics, Law, Morality: Essays by V. S. Soloviev*, ed. and trans. by Vladimir Wozniuk (New Haven: Yale University Press, 2000).

19   *Untranslated Collected Works of Vladimir Soloviev (SSVS)*, Vol. 13, p. 188, as quoted by Gregory Flazov, "Vladimir Solovyov and the Idea of Papacy," *Communio*, 24, Spring 1997, p. 130.

20   Cf. *Politics, Law, Morality: Essays by V. S. Soloviev*, ed. and trans. by Vladimir Wozniuk (New Haven: Yale University Press, 2000).

Treason of the Intellectuals

1   Julian Benda, *La trahison des clercs* (Paris: B. Grasset, 1927). Trans. by Richard Aldington as *The Betrayal of the Intellectuals* (New York: Morrow & Co., 1928).

2   As reported by Jamie Whyte, *Wall Street Journal* (February 13, 2012, p. A-17).

3   Pierre Manent, *Democracy without Nations: The Fate of Self-Government in Europe*, translated from the French with an introduction by Paul Seaton (Wilmington, Del.: ISI Books, 2007).

4   Ibid., p. 33.

5   Jocelyn Maclure, Charles Taylor, *Secularism and Freedom of Conscience*, translated by Jane Marie Todd (Cambridge, Mass.: Harvard University Press, 2011).

6   Ibid., p. 2.

7   Ibid., p. 3.

8   Ibid., p. 11.

9   Ibid., p. 21

10   Marcello Pera, *Why We Should Call Ourselves Christians* (New York: Encounter Books, 2011).

11   Ibid., pp. 8–9.

12   Ibid., p. 9.

13   Ibid.

14   Brad S. Gregory, *The Unintended Reformation: How a Religious Revolution Secularized Society* (Cambridge, Mass.: The Belknap Press at Harvard University, 2012).

15 Ibid., p. 383.
16 Ibid., p. 386.
17 Ibid., p. 158.

Two Treatises on the Acquisition and Use of Power

1   Rémi Brague, The Legend of the Middle Ages: Philosophical Explorations of Medieval Christianity, Judaism, and Islam, trans. by Lydia G. Cochrane. (Chicago: University of Chicago Press, 2009).

2   Adrian Goldsworthy, How Rome Fell: Death of a Superpower (New Haven: Yale University Press, 2009).

3   Paul A. Rahe, Montesquieu and the Logic of Liberty (New Haven: Yale University Press, 2009).

4   Bertrand de Jouvenal, On Power: Its Nature and the History of Its Growth, with a preface by D. W. Brogan; trans. by J. F. Huntington (New York: The Viking Press, 1949).

5   Pierre Manent, Democracy without Nations: The Fate of Self-Government in Europe, trans. from the French by Paul Seaton (Wilmington, Del.: ISI Books, 2007).

6   Paraphrased by D. W. Brogan in his preface, pp. xvi–xvii.

7   Ibid., pp. 11–12.

8   Ibid., p. 12.

9   Ibid.

10 Ibid., p. 157.

11 Ibid., p. 171.

12 Ibid., p. 11.

13 Ibid.

14 Ibid., p. 380.

15 Yves R. Simon, The Community of the Free, trans. from the original French by Willard R. Trask (Lanham, MD: University Press of America, 1984).

16 Simon, op. cit., p. 149.

17 "The real question is whether democracy can lead to totalitarianism, whether a democratic regime can develop into a totalitarian regime, whether the democratic state may happen to work in such a way as to bring about the elimination of democracy and the establishment of totalitarianism." (Simon, p. 150.)

18 De Jouvenal, op. cit., p. 261.

19 Richard Pipes, Property and Freedom (New York: Alfred A. Knopf, 1999).

20 Pipes, op. cit., p. 229.

21 Ibid., p. 287.

22 Ibid., p. 288.

23 de Jouvenal, op. cit., p. 373.

24 Ibid., p. 377.

25 Ibid.

26 F. A. Hayek, The Road to Serfdom (Chicago: University of Chicago Press, 1944). Because of a paper shortage in England, Hayek with the aid a friend sought publication in North America. In the United States, the manuscript was turned down by three major publishers before it was accepted for publication by the

University of Chicago Press. Given a glowing review in the London Sunday Times Book Review, the initial printing of 2,000 copies was soon increased to 20,000. By the time the 50th anniversary edition was issued, the book had sold 81,000 copies in hardback and 175,000 in paperback. The Reader's Digest had distributed an additional 600,000 copies in condensed form.

27   Hayek, op. cit , p. 4

28   For a valuable discussion of the impact of the Vienna Circle on the economic and political theorists of the day, see Malachi H. Hacohen, Karl Popper: The Formative Years, 1902–1945: Politics and Philosophy in Interwar Vienna (Cambridge: Cambridge University Press, 2000).

29   Cf. John H. Hallowell, "Positivism," Chap. 9 in Main Currents in Modern Political Thought (New York: Henry Holt & Co., 1950), pp. 289–327.

30   Ludwig von Mises, Socialism: An Economic and Sociological Analysis, trans. from the 1932 German edition by J. Kahane (New York: The Macmillan Co., 1845). Von Mises was writing before the full effects of socialism were felt on the Continent.

31   Hallowell, op. cit., pp. 225–226.

32   Hallowell, op. cit., p. 226.

33   Ludwig von Mises, in Collectivist Economic Planning, ed. by Friedrich von Hayek (London: Routledge, 1935).

34   Ibid., p. 111.

35   Hacohen, op. cit., p. 485.

36   Ibid.

37   Hacohen, op. cit., p. 507.

38   F. A. Hayek, The Fatal Conceit: The Errors of Socialism, in The Collected Works of F. A. Hayek, ed. by W. W. Bartley III (Chicago: University of Chicago Press, 1989), p. 103.

39   Cf. Murray N. Rothbard, Biography of Ludwig von Mises (1881–1973), Ludwig von Mises Institute, home page.

40   Hayek, Road to Serfdom, p. xliii.

41   Ibid., p. 149.

42   Ibid., p. 150.

43   We saw this principle illustrated in the 2008 elections in the United States where Blacks and Hispanics voted as a block. About five million more people voted in the November 2008 presidential election than four years earlier, with the newly enfranchised accounting for almost the entire increase. About two million more Blacks and Hispanics and 600,000 additional Asians went to the polls (Wall Street Journal, 7/21/09, p. A, 3).

44   Hayek, Road to Serfdom, p. 152.

45   Ibid., pp. 152–153.

46   Ibid., p. 153.

47   Ibid.

48   Ibid., p. 291.

49   Ibid., p. 161.

50   F. A. Hayek, Law, Legislation and Liberty, 3 vols. (Chicago: University of Chicago Press, 1973, 1976, 1979).

51   Hayek, The Fatal Conceit, p. 29.

52 Ibid., p. 32.

53 Ibid., p. 54.

54 Cf. Von Mises, "Preface," in Bureaucracy (New Haven: Yale University Press, 1944).

Property as a Condition of Liberty

1 Plato modifies this position somewhat in the *Laws*, when he writes, "Let the citizens at once distribute their land and houses, and not till their land in common, since a community of goods goes beyond their proposed origin, and nurture and education" [*The Dialogues of Plato, Laws*,740, trans. B. Jowett, Vol. II, (New York: Random House, 1937)].

2 Aristotle, *Politics,* 2263, a 15–16.

3 Marcus Tullius Cicero, *On Duties*, trans. Walter Miller (Cambridge, Mass.: Harvard University Press, 1997), I, p. 21.

4 Ibid., p. 22.

5 Ibid., p. 49.

6 Ibid., II, p. 73.

7 Ibid., II, p. 78.

8 Ibid., I, p. 92.

9 The complexity of adjudicating law governing intellectual property is seen in *Eldred* v. *Ashcroft*, 537 U.S. 186 (2003), also cited below.

10 Karl Marx and Friedrich Engels, *The Communist Manifesto* (New York: International Publishers, 1935), pp. 42–43.

11 John Stuart Mill, *Principles of Political Economy* (Oxford: Oxford University Press, 1994), cf. Chaps. I, II.

12 John Rawls, *A Theory of Justice* (Cambridge, Mass.: Harvard University Press, 1971).

13 Ibid., pp. 1010–1102 [this should be checked: 1010–1012?]

14 *Eldred* v. *Ashcroft*, 537 U.S. 186 (2003).

15 Pierre Joseph Proudhon, *Q'est-ce qua la Propriete?* Trans. Benjamin B. R. Tucker as *What is Property?* (New York: H. Fertio, 1966), p. 147.

16 John Rawls, *The Law of Peoples: With the Idea of Public Reason Revisited* (Cambridge: Harvard University Press, 1999), p. 9.

17 Pierre Manent, *Democracy without Nations: The Fate of Self-Government in Europe*, trans. from the French by Paul Seaton (Wilmington, Del.: ISI Books, 2009).

18 Ibid., p. 66.

19 Richard Pipes, *Property and Freedom* (New York: Alfred A. Knopf, 1999).

20 As quoted by Pipes, p. 229.

21 Ibid., p. 229.

22 Ibid., p. 283.

23 Cf. Douglas North and E. P. Thomas, *The Rise of the Western World* (Cambridge, Mass.: Cambridge University Press, 1973). Also Douglas North, *Structure and Change in Economic History* (New York: Norton, 1981); Tom Bethel, *The Noblest Triumph* (New York: St. Martin's Press, 1998).

24 *Eldred v. Ashcroft*, 537 U.S. 186 (2003).

Tolerance: Virtue or Vice

1   Oswald Spengler, *The Decline of the West* (New York: A. A. Knopf, 1926–28).

2   Pierre Manent, *Democracy without Nations: The Fate of Self-Government in Europe*, trans. Paul Seaton (Wilmington, Del.: ISI Books, 2007).

3   The most effective instrument for the creation of a beneficent attitude to Islam lies within the university presses that publish often questionable scholarship produced by holders of university chairs endowed by Islamic donors. Islamic-American organizations have become adept at using the op-ed pages of major newspapers and even U.S. agencies to advance a benevolent interpretation of Islam. The U.S. Department of Homeland Security distributed in 2009, without a publication date, a 43-page pamphlet entitled, "Violent Islamic Extremism: A Primer." Apparently it was produced to persuade the public that it has nothing to fear from a peaceful Islam. The enemy, we are assured, is not the religion of Islam but a global network of extremists who misinterpret the text of Islam. Authors of the pamphlet, drawing upon what they claim is reliable academic research, apparently hold that they are in a position to distinguish authentic Islam from its heresies.

4   Cf. *Early Modern Skepticism and the Origins of Toleration*, ed. by Alan Levin (Lanham, MD: Lexington Books, 1998).

5   Johann Wolfgang von Goethe, *Maxims and Reflections* (London: Penguin Classics, 1999), p. 116.

6   Titus Livius, Preface to his *History* (Cambridge, Mass.: Loeb Classical Library, Harvard University Press, 1924), p. I.5.

Responsibility: Recognition and Limits

1   *Wall Street Journal*, August 26, 2006, p. A-3.

2   News release, Southasia.oneworld.net, September 4, 2006.

3   Cf. Hywel David Lewis, *Philosophy* XXII (84), January 1948, p. 47. See also Joel Feinberg, "Collective Responsibility," *Journal of Philosophy*, LXV (21), November 1968, pp. 674–688 and Virginia Held, "Can a Random Collection of Individuals be Morally Responsible," *Journal of Philosophy*, LXVII, July 1970, pp. 471–481.

4   Otto Von Gierke, *Political Theory of the Middle Ages*, trans F. W. Maitland (Cambridge, England: Cambridge University Press, 1900).

5   Brian Tierney, *Religion, Law and the Growth of Constitutional Thought, 1150–1650* (Cambridge: Cambridge University Press, 1982), p. 23.

6   Peter A. French, *Collective and Corporate Responsibility* (New York: Columbia University Press, 1984, p. 39).

7   Jackson said, "We know the Nazi party was not put into power by a majority of the German vote. We know that it came to power by an evil alliance between the most extreme of the Nazi revolutionaries, the most unrestrained of the German reactionaries and the most aggressive of the German militarists," in: Suzanne Brown-Fleming, *The Holocaust and the Catholic Conscience: Cardinal Aloisius Muench and the Guilt Question in Germany* (South Bend: University of Notre Dame Press, 2006), p. 149.

8   Ibid.

9 Ibid., p. 16.
10 Ibid., p. 148.
11 Emile Durkheim, *Rules of Sociological Method*, trans. S. Soloway and J. Mueller, ed. Carlin (New York: Free Press, 1964), p. 7.
12 Karl Jaspers, *The Question of German Guilt*, trans. E. B. Ashton (New York: Capricorn Books, 1961). (First published by Dial Press, Inc., 1947.)
13 Ibid., pp. 31–32.
14 Ibid., p. 117.
15 Ibid., p. 32.
16 Ibid., p. 41.
17 Muench was subsequently named Apostolic Visitor to Germany in 1946 at the request of the American occupation forces, and in 1959 hc was appointed Papal Nuncio to Germany. In 1959 he was named Cardinal. Cf. "The Cardinal Muench Papers," Catholic University of America Archives.
18 "One World in Charity," A Pastoral, Lent 1946, p. 9. Text provided courtesy Jordan Patty, Archivist, The Catholic University of America.
19 Secretary of State, James F. Byrnes, in his statement of December 11, 1945, defining official policies for Germany. "In terms of world supply, liberated areas must enjoy a higher priority than Germany throughout this first postwar winter," quoted by Muench, p. 9.
20 Margaret Truman, *Harry S. Truman* (New York: William Morrow & Co., 1973) p. 265.
21 Dorothy Sayers, "The Lost Tools of Learning,"1947 Lecture at Oxford University, p. 12. Available at www.brccs.org/Sayers

The Aristotelian Element in Boethius's Understanding of the Trinity

1 Boethius, Anicius Manlius Severinus. *The Theological Tractates: The Trinity is One God, Not Three Gods*, trans. H. F. Stewart and E. K. Rand, and *The Consolation of Philosophy*, trans. by "I. T." (1609), revised by H. F. Stewart (London: William Heineman, 1918), p. 3. (All future page references are to this edition of the two works.)
2 *Consolation*, p. 82.
3 *De Trinitate*, p.79.
4 Ibid., p. 79.
5 Ibid., p. 83.
6 Ibid., p. 85.

Benedict on the Nature of Scientific Enquiry

1 Joseph Ratzinger, Pope Benedict XVI, *Jesus of Nazareth*, trans. from the German by Adrian Walker (New York: Doubleday, 2007), p. 319.
2 Ibid., p. xxii.
3 Carroll Stuhmueller, C.P., "Vatican II and Biblical Criticism," in Jude P. Dougherty, ed. *The Impact of Vatican II* (St. Louis: B. Herder, 1966), p. 28.
4 Ibid., p. xvi.

5   Ibid., p. xxi.
6   Ibid., p. xxii.

Moderate Islam

1   Bernard Lewis, *What Went Wrong?: The Clash between Islam and Modernity in the Middle East* (Cambridge, MA: Harvard University Press, 2002).
2   Rémi Brague, *The Legend of the Middle Ages: Philosophical Explorations of Medieval Christianity, Judaism, and Islam*, trans. by Lydia G. Cochrane (Chicago: University of Chicago Press, 2009).
3   Ignaz Goldziher, *Introduction to Islamic Theology and Law*, trans. by Andras and Ruth Hamori (Princeton: Princeton University Press, 1981).
4   Brague, op. cit., p. 21.
5   Goldziher, op. cit., p. 32.
6   Goldziher, op. cit., pp. 37–38.
7   Goldziher, op. cit., p. 68.
8   Ali A. Allawi, *The Crisis of Islamic Civilization* (New Haven: Yale University Press, 2009).
9   Samuel P. Huntington, *The Clash of Civilizations and the Remaking of the World Order* (New York: Simon and Schuster, 1995).